TURTLES

An Extraordinary Natural History 245 Million Years in the Making

By Carl J. Franklin
Illustrations by David C. Killpack

Voyageur Press

On the cover:
Ornate box turtle (*Terrapene ornata*)
David C. Killpack

On the back cover:
Top: African spurred tortoise
(*Geochelone sulcata*)

Bottom left: Black-breasted leaf
turtle (*Geoemyda spengleri*)

Bottom right: Common spider
tortoise (*Pyxis arachnoides*).
Matt Vaughn

On the spine: Slider (*Trachemys* sp.)

On the frontispiece:
Parker's snake-necked turtle
(*Macrochelodina parkeri*)

On the title pages:
Mexican giant musk turtle
(*Staurotypus triporcatus*) hatchling

On the title pages, small photo:
African spurred tortoise
(*Geochelone sulcata*)

Opposite the table of contents:
Yucatan box turtle
(*Terrapene carolina yucatana*)

On the table of contents:
Yellow-spotted river turtle
(*Podocnemis unifilis*)

First published in 2007 by Voyageur Press, an imprint of MBI Publishing Company, Galtier Plaza, Suite 200, 380 Jackson Street, St. Paul, MN 55101 USA

Text © 2007 by Carl J. Franklin
Photos © 2007 by Carl J. Franklin unless otherwise noted
Maps and illustrations © 2007 by David C. Killpack

The information in this book is true and complete to the best of our knowledge. All recommendations are made without any guarantee on the part of the author or Publisher, who also disclaim any liability incurred in connection with the use of this data or specific details.

We recognize, further, that some words, model names, and designations mentioned herein are the property of the trademark holder. We use them for identification purposes only. This is not an official publication.

MBI Publishing Company titles are also available at discounts in bulk quantity for industrial or sales-promotional use. For details write to Special Sales Manager at MBI Publishing Company, Galtier Plaza, Suite 200, 380 Jackson Street, St. Paul, MN 55101 USA

Library of Congress Cataloging-in-Publication Data

Franklin, Carl J.
  Turtles : an extraordinary natural history 245 million years in the making / by Carl J. Franklin ; Illustrations by David C. Killpack.
    p. cm.
  Includes index.
  ISBN-13: 978-0-7603-2981-8 (hardbound w/ jacket)
  ISBN-10: 0-7603-2981-8 (hardbound w/ jacket) 1. Turtles. I. Title.
QL666.C5F64 2007
597.92'4—dc22
                              2006027181

Edited by Danielle J. Ibister
Designed by Sara Holle

Printed in China

Acknowledgments

This book would not have been possible without the assistance and generosity of several individuals: Jonathan A. Campbell, chairman of the Department of Biology and director of the Amphibian and Reptile Diversity Research Center at the University of Texas at Arlington; Marco Natera of the Universidad Nacional Experimental Rómulo Gallegos; Peter C. H. Pritchard and Tim Walsh of the Chelonian Research Institute; Gilson Rivas of Museo de Historia Natural La Salle, Caracas, Venezuela; and Jeffry A. Seigel of the Natural History Museum of Los Angeles County. All of the aforementioned generously allowed the use of their museum facilities as well as access to reference materials and specimens under their care. Collette Adams, curator of amphibians and reptiles at the Gladys Porter Zoo; Luis Sigler of the Dallas World Aquarium; Diane Barber, curator of Ectotherms, and Rick Hudson, director of Conservation at the Fort Worth Zoo; Dave Collins, curator of forests at the Tennessee Aquarium; Saul Gutierrez and Jack Hoopia of Terrario del Parque del Este, Caracas, Venezuela; Dwight Lawson, vice president of Animal Programs and Science at Zoo Atlanta; and Rob Macinness of Glades Herp all provided photographic opportunities of specimens under their care.

Key insights into the functioning biology of the Fitzroy River turtle would have been difficult, if not impossible, without the advice and assistance of Dr. John Legler from the Department of Biology at the University of Utah. In addition, Dr. Jon Anderson; Dr. Peter Antich, professor of Advanced Radiological Sciences at the University of Texas Southwestern Medical Center and director; and the staff of the Positron Emission Tomography facility at University of Texas Southwestern Medical Center at Dallas were immensely helpful.

Additional expressions of gratitude for the use of photographs are necessary for Shreyas Krishnan of the University of Texas at Arlington and Matt Vaughn of the Fort Worth Zoo herpetarium for providing photographs of rare species for this project.

Special thanks are in order for the author's wife and son, Jacqueline and James, as well as the illustrator's wife, Sierra, for the patience and support they provided during this project.

Contents

*The red coloration in the head of breeding male painted terrapins (*Callagur borneoensis*) is due to increased blood circulation.*

Introduction

Millions of years before the first humans walked the earth or swam its waters, turtles had already mastered both elements. Representing an ancient reptilian lineage at its zenith, these reptiles remain virtually unchanged from their early ancestors that first appeared some 245 million years ago. Their shelled form, behaviors, and ecology have secured turtles as worthy contenders within the grand scheme of natural selection.

This evolutionary success places turtles among the most widely recognized animals on the planet. Even the fossils left by ancestral chelonians are readily identifiable as turtles. Today, approximately three hundred species of turtles inhabit virtually every type of habitat, except polar, and can be found on every continent except Antarctica.

Despite more than 200 million years of evolutionary success, turtles currently face a threat to their very existence. Humans have exploited the environment and reproduced unlike any species of vertebrate in recorded history. This behavior has been the harbinger of extinction for many species of plants and animals. If turtles continue to disappear from nature, the extinction of these fascinating creatures is imminent.

Many turtles are enduring a losing battle to maintain their tenuous extant status. This is not simply a theory, but a fact that we must embrace if we are to alter this alarming trend.

The threats facing turtles are numerous. A thorough description of these factors would easily exceed the scope of this book. Fortunately, several organizations have devoted their energy, time, resources, and spirit toward trying to save the turtles we still have. A listing of these groups is included in the appendix. I encourage anyone interested in learning more about turtle conservation to contact these organizations.

The intent of this book is to provide a glimpse into the colorful and extraordinary diversity found among turtles. Their natural history, ecology, biogeography, interesting behaviors, and constant struggle for survival are some of the topics explored. I am constantly amazed, enchanted, excited, and even inspired by these beautiful and fascinating reptiles. I hope this book will inspire you to learn more about these shelled creatures and to help them survive the twenty-first century.

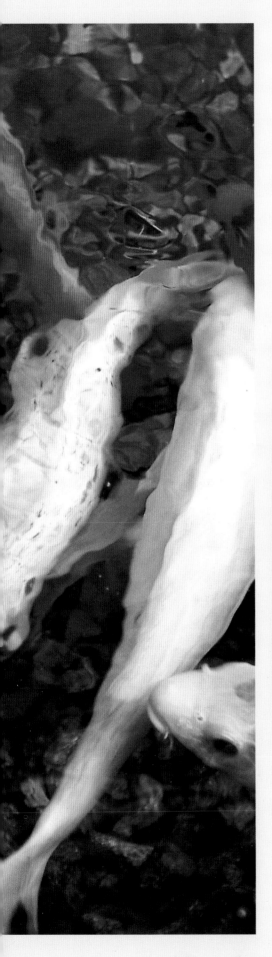

Part One
The Life and Lifestyle of Turtles

*The black-breasted leaf turtle (*Geoemyda spengleri*) inhabits moist evergreen forests and leads a primarily terrestrial life, entering streams on occasion.*

***Left:** Red-eared sliders (*Trachemys scripta elegans*) are the most common pet turtle. Here a mature female swims among koi.*

Chapter 1
Chelonian Taxonomy, Form, and Function

As with most organisms, common names for turtles are used more often than technical or scientific labels. These common names vary from country to country. Slider is a common name widely used in the United States for the freshwater turtle *Trachemys scripta*. The indigenous inhabitants of eastern Honduras and Nicaragua call the same species of turtle Kuswa.

Oftentimes, common names are applied to entire groups of organisms and these also vary between countries. For example, the term "terrapin" is used frequently in the Eastern Hemisphere to refer to any turtles living in fresh water or on land. The American usage of the word is restricted to a specific type of turtle that occurs along the Atlantic coastline of the United States. Likewise, in the Eastern Hemisphere, "tortoise" is a term used for a wide variety of turtles, including aquatic species. However, the proper usage of "tortoise" in the United States is in specific reference to terrestrial turtles belonging to the family Testudinidae.

The Asian leaf turtle (Cyclemys dentata) inhabits shallow streams and consumes a wide variety of food items, including plants and small animals.

To minimize confusion, scientific names are used. This classification provides a clear and accurate way to label every known plant and animal. The names used in scientific categorization are rooted in Latin and Greek. They always appear in italics, which allows for universal recognition. The use of two names to identify organisms is the basis of binomial nomenclature, a system founded by the eighteenth-century naturalist Carolus Linnaeus.

Taxonomy

Understanding the fundamentals of chelonian taxonomy is simple. In the most basic of taxonomic terms, every species of turtle belongs to a genus, which in turn belongs to a particular family. Families comprise the order that makes up the class and phylum, belonging to a kingdom.

Basic Taxonomic Classification for the Mexican Box Turtle (*Terrapene carolina mexicana*)

Kingdom: Animalia
Phylum: Chordata
Class: Anapsida
Order: Testudines
Suborder: Cryptodira
Family: Emydidae
Genus: *Terrapene*
Species: *carolina*
Subspecies: *mexicana*

*The bridge connects the upper shell, or carapace, to the bottom shell, or plastron. Pictured here is the bridge of a painted turtle (*Chrysemys picta*).*

Physical Features

Skeletal System

Like all reptiles, turtles have a well-developed skeletal system. However, the chelonian skeletal system comes with a major distinction: the shell. During embryonic development, turtles undergo a fundamental departure from the standard vertebrate plan. The bones that bridge the gap between the axillary and appendicular skeleton, the pectoral and pelvic girdles, develop within the main body cavity created by the ribcage. In other words, if you had developed as a turtle does, your clavicle, scapula, and pelvis would be inside your ribcage along with all your other organs! As you have likely observed, most turtles can withdraw their arms, legs, tail, head, and neck to some degree within their shell. Of course, your ribcage would need to be considerably larger to hold all these extra components, as the shell is in the turtles. This major modification to the body plan provides a great deal of protection. Furthermore, the turtle's ribcage is encased in dermal bone to the point that the shell itself bears little resemblance to its primitive ribcage state.

A turtle's shell comprises three major components: the carapace, the bridge, and the plastron. The carapace constitutes the upper part of the shell and is essentially a fusion of the ribs, vertebrae, and

Because of the shell, turtles have a more distinctive skeletal system than any other group of vertebrates.

dermal bone. The carapace connects to the bottom half of the shell (the plastron) by the bridge.

Turtle shells consist of 59 to 61 bones that, in most instances, are covered with sections of horny keratin called scutes. Scutes are rigid scales that overlie and protect the bones of the shell. They reduce moisture evaporation, providing an added amount of protection.

While this type of shell is the norm for a vast majority of turtles, some shells are covered with leathery flesh or flesh impregnated with pieces of bone called osteoderms. The Fly River turtle (*Carettochelys insculpta*), the Central American river turtle (*Dermatemys mawii*), the soft-shelled turtles (family Trionychidae), and the leatherback sea turtle (*Dermochelys coriacea*) all possess a carapace covered by a layer of flesh instead of keratinized scutes.

Not unlike the vaulted arches used to support ceilings in cathedrals and stadiums, the turtle's domed shell provides an incredible amount of support. Some turtles that inhabit the same waters as

crocodilians are equipped with a hard carapace and plastron joined by a buttress-like bridge. The river cooter (*Pseudemys concinna*) has this type of shell. The shell's design provides rigid support against the incredible crushing power that is generated by the jaws of an alligator or crocodile. While some crocodilians are certainly capable of crushing the shell of just about any species of aquatic turtle, a strong shell is undoubtedly a useful feature for turtles.

The Central American giant musk turtle not only has a thick and sturdy shell, but it has three ridges running lengthwise along the carapace called keels. The keels continue to grow and become more prominent as the turtle matures. These keels not only improve the structural integrity of the shell, but also reduce the amount of surface area for a crocodilian to grasp a wriggling turtle.

Movable hinges have proven to be an improvement on the already successful concept of the shell. Many turtles that have hinged shells are capable of closing either the posterior portion of the plastron,

The raised longitudinal keels on the carapace of the Mexican giant musk turtle (Staurotypus triporcatus) become more prominent as the turtle matures. These ridges reinforce the sturdy shell and may be a useful deterrent against the powerful jaws of a crocodile.

Operating in the same manner as a drawbridge, the plastral hinge helps this Indochinese box turtle (Cuora galbinifrons) keep out unwanted guests.

the anterior portion of the plastron, or both. Some of the forest- and savanna-dwelling species of African tortoises have a moveable hinge located on the posterior portion of their carapace that allows them to move the rear portion of the shell.

Hinges help provide a means of defense against predators. Of course, many turtles close the front of the shell by moving a hinge on the anterior portion of the plastron upward and toward the carapace. Instead of using a hinge to close the shell, the giant musk turtles (*Staurotypus* spp.) flex the anterior portion of their plastrons outward. By doing so, they are able to withdraw their large heads within their shells. In the females of some species, a posterior-oriented hinge or a flexible suture between the plastral seams facilitates the passage of large eggs. Some female tortoises lack a flexible plastron, but still deliver large eggs. For these species, a notch in the posterior portion of the carapace provides room for an egg to pass.

Depending on the species, the carapace may be domed or almost entirely flat. This variation correlates to the type of lifestyle maintained by any given species. Most aquatic turtles possess a streamlined body form, while terrestrial species typically have a domed carapace.

Turtles belonging to the families Carrettochelyidae and Trionychidae possess a flattened carapace covered in leathery flesh instead of keratinized scutes. These turtles are also adept at burying themselves beneath sand, fine gravel, and other aquatic substrate material. Since their shells are relatively flat and somewhat flexible, they can conceal themselves efficiently. Upon reaching the bottom of a body of water, they shuffle their plastrons back and forth into the sand and kick up substrate with their hind feet. Many shuffle backward into the oncoming substrate. The only visible indications of a turtle, once covered, are often two eyes and a snout.

In the case of the leatherback sea turtle (*Dermochelys coriacea*), the bony elements in the plastron are reduced to such an extent that nesting females have been accidentally impaled on driftwood during their nocturnal sojourns to beachfront nesting grounds. The carapace of the leatherback is different from all other turtles. Instead of having a solid shell with a carapace containing 59 to 61 bones, the leatherback's large carapace is made of thick, leathery flesh impregnated with a mosaic of thousands of tiny bones. These shells are challenging for museum curators to prepare as dry specimens because they contain a seemingly never-ending supply of oil that drips for years.

When discussing turtles that have a reduction of the bony elements in their shells, another species deserves mention. The African pancake tortoise (*Malacochersus tornieri*) of Kenya and Tanzania resides in the boulder-strewn habitats of scrub forests. This tortoise utilizes its flexible shell to exploit the cracks and crevices of its habitat for maximum protection against predators. The pancake tortoise has a lighter and more flexible shell than that of any other species of tortoise. Its shell allows the turtle to move rapidly in its rocky habitat with a fair amount of agility.

Shell

The main reason these reptiles have a shell is for protection. Although the chelonian shell is not strong enough to protect them entirely against all predators, it is an incredible structure that is capable of greatly enhancing a turtle's chances of survival.

Shells protect turtles from more than just predators. One naturally occurring event that directly affects wildlife and alters ecological systems is a wildfire. In the pine forest of eastern Honduras, I encountered an interesting brown wood turtle (*Rhinoclemmys annulata*) that had fire-scarred limbs and a badly scorched shell. Aside from the cosmetic damage, the turtle appeared to be in good health. In fact, the turtle is still part of my personal live collection. Presumably, the turtle survived the blaze by withdrawing itself tightly within its shell and pushing as deeply into the ground as it could.

Tough shells have repeatedly proven themselves effective protection against various carnivores. However, herbivores may have influenced the evolution of shells among some terrestrial species. As recently as two hundred years ago, the ornate box turtle (*Terrapene ornata*) shared a landscape with millions of bison. The hoofed beast occupied enormous amounts of land throughout the central United States. As the bison grazed, they produced a significant amount of waste that attracted prey such as flies and beetles. Box turtles find these insects to be irresistible. Unlike other prairie inhabitants such as rattlesnakes and prairie dogs, box turtles have no means by which they can threaten or race away from an animal that is about to step on them. One can only imagine if more box turtles were merely pressed into the ground or suffered broken shells after being

*The shell of this spiny turtle (*Heosemys spinosa*) could prove an extreme challenge for even the hungriest of snakes to swallow.*

stepped on by the roaming buffalo.

Some turtle hatchlings have shells bearing keels, pointed marginal scutes, and other interesting ornamentations. However, these features often disappear entirely following the onset of maturity. The spiny turtle (*Heosemys spinosa*) is an exceptional example of a turtle with an ornamented shell. When viewed from above, juveniles of this species resemble a star-like cog or a misplaced gear. Presumably, these features afford some protection against predators. Perhaps the prospect of consuming a spiny, star-like turtle is unpleasant enough that most snakes decide against swallowing one.

Skull

Among vertebrates, turtles possess a unique skull. One of the fundamental factors for establishing basic taxonomic arrangements among reptiles is the presence and number of temporal fossae. Temporal fossae are openings in the skull left by the formation of structural features called temporal arches. Temporal arches provide points of insertion and articulation for muscles and tendons. With this in mind, the unique nature of a turtle's skull is easier to understand. Turtles are the only living amniotic vertebrate without temporal openings in the skull.

Although the chelonian skull lacks temporal arches, it still has accommodations for necessary muscles, tendons, blood vessels, and nerves. Not only do all turtles lack temporal openings in the skull, but they also have a skull with a solid, bony roof that overlies the jaw muscles.

Another unique feature of turtle skulls is that they do not have teeth. Instead of teeth, chelonians have a bony cusp. This oral structure varies from species to species. Many cusps are beak-like, others are serrated, and some have downward pointing projections along the roof of the mouth and throat. Despite the fact that cusps can and often do aid in feeding, they are not teeth. Instead, a layer of keratin lines a cusp that often has an edge suitable for cutting or slicing vegetative matter.

Feet

Turtle feet are significant to chelonian anatomy and provide insight into the ecological niche occupied by any given species. Some of the many necessary functions performed by the turtle's feet include climbing, swimming, walking amid rocky cliffs, providing propulsion while swimming, digging tunnels, securing a grip onto the shells of females while mating, covering the face, and maintaining traction in slippery mud. As one can imagine, turtle feet are diverse and allow chelonians to occupy various environmental niches.

Tail

Of all the living reptiles, turtles demonstrate a significant amount of tail reduction. While a short tail is the norm for turtles, there are exceptions. Snapping turtles and big-headed turtles both have considerably longer tails that are approximately the same length as the shell. In many instances, these long tails have proven essential to the ecology of these species.

The cloaca is at the base of the tail, and the reproductive organs are within the tail. Because the male's tail houses the penis, it is usually longer and wider at the base than that of the female.

Male musk turtles (family Kinosternidae) have a keratinized projection on the tip of their tails. The male uses the keratinized tip to assist holding the female's tail in position during mating. Male Mexican giant musk turtles (family Staurotypidae)

These skulls illustrate the skeletal diversity among chelonians. Shown here, from left to right, are the skulls of the green sea turtle (Chelonia mydas mydas); *the matamata* (Chelus fimbriatus); *the big-headed Amazon River turtle* (Peltocephalus dumerilianus); *the painted terrapin* (Callagur borneoensis); *and the Asiatic soft-shelled turtle* (Amyda cartilaginea).

Fitzroy River Turtle
Rheodytes leukops (Legler & Cann, 1980)

All turtles breathe air with their lungs. Although there are some supplemental means of respiration found in chelonians, in no species has it reached the extent of modification as within this white-eyed stream diver.

Rheodytes practices a form of respiration known as ***cloacal gill respiration.***

To accomplish this feat, water is pumped in and out of pouches known as cloacal bursae via the muscles of the inguinal pocket at a rate of 15 to 60 times per minute.

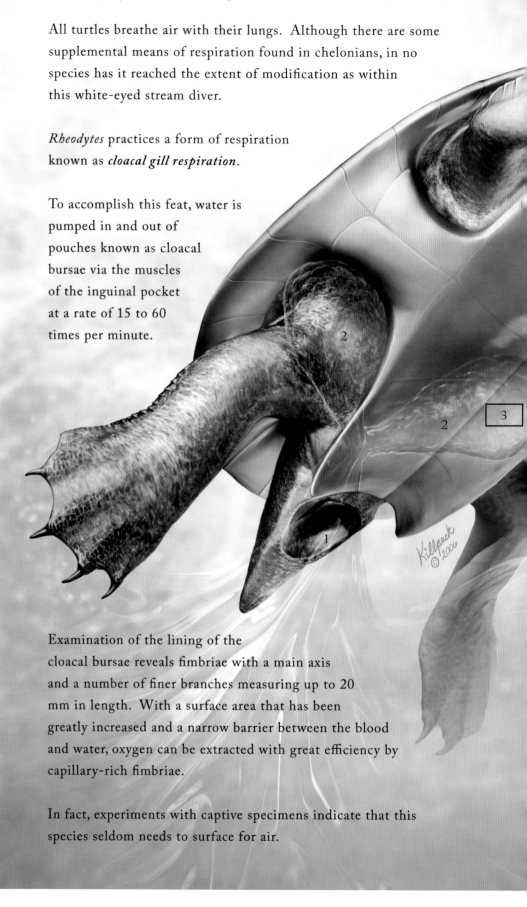

Examination of the lining of the cloacal bursae reveals fimbriae with a main axis and a number of finer branches measuring up to 20 mm in length. With a surface area that has been greatly increased and a narrow barrier between the blood and water, oxygen can be extracted with great efficiency by capillary-rich fimbriae.

In fact, experiments with captive specimens indicate that this species seldom needs to surface for air.

David C. Killpack

1. Muscular cloacal orifice where water enters the system.

2. Paired cloacal bursae expand and contract via the muscles of the inguinal pocket.

3. Long fimbriae lining the inner surface of the bursae are highly vascular and efficiently extract oxygen from the water.

sometimes insert the tip of their tail into the female's cloaca just prior to copulation. Given that, females of this species are much larger than the males. This act not only assists males in aligning themselves, but also helps them locate the female's cloaca.

Mature male sea turtles not only have a longer tail than the females, but the tail is also somewhat prehensile. A prehensile tail is useful for gripping the female during mating, as well as for covering her cloaca, which prevents interruptions from other anxious males.

Respiration

All amniotic vertebrates (reptiles, birds, and mammals) use lungs for breathing. Most draw air in and out of the lungs using a diaphragm, which is a muscle that contracts and relaxes involuntarily. Whenever these animals breathe, you see the body moving. However, unlike other amniotes, turtles do not possess a diaphragm. Even if a turtle had a diaphragm, the rigid structure of the shell would prevent the turtle from moving its body (i.e., expanding its ribs) while breathing. Instead, turtles must move their limbs or neck to fill their lungs with air. They also use muscles connected to the pleural cavity that surrounds the lungs to assist with breathing. When these muscles contract, the lungs expand and fill with air. Likewise, muscular movements allow the turtle to exhale as well. While some turtles have this layer of muscles surrounding their lungs, others use special muscles situated between their limbs and lungs. This characteristic is why frightened turtles often make a hissing sound when they retract their head into their shell. The audible hiss results from all the air that is forced out of the lungs.

Aside from using lungs to supply their bodies with oxygen, some turtles have evolved to have additional means that make breathing more efficient. Several aquatic species have the ability to stay underwater for extended periods without surfacing for air. Some of these turtles remain submerged by performing buccopharyngeal breathing, in which they gulp water into their mouths and passing it out of their nostrils. In this mode of respiration, oxygenated water passes along the capillary-rich tissue near the surface of the flesh inside the neck. The surface of this skin contains innervations of capillaries that allow oxygen to enter directly into the bloodstream. This form of respiration permits many species to remain underwater longer than if they were solely dependent upon their lungs. Since turtles have the ability to meet their requirement for oxygen without leaving the water, they are able to regulate their buoyancy. The turtle remains quietly on the bottom, where it can locate prey or seek shelter.

The alternative modes of respiration for animals with lungs are interesting, to say the least. One species of turtle has gone beyond mere buccopharyngeal respiration to remain underwater. The Fitzroy River turtle (*Rheodytes leukops*) of Australia moves richly oxygenated water in and out of its cloaca. Water is pumped directly into two vascularized bursae, or pouches, that are designed to absorb oxygen directly from the water. Elongated and thread-like fimbriae enriched with capillaries line the inner surface of the bursae. *Rheodytes* uses muscles near the point of insertion of the hind legs, called inguinal muscles, to pump water in and out of the bursae.

Incredibly, this species receives more of its required oxygen from the water than through its lungs. Laboratory experiments have demonstrated that *Rheodytes* can remain submerged underwater for up to nine hours.

While *Rheodytes* demonstrates the most fascinating use of cloacal bursae, other aquatic turtles also have cloacal bursae. While some of these turtles use the bursae to respire, they can also use them to enhance buoyancy control.

Sensory Realm

For the most part, turtles are visually oriented creatures that rely heavily on their eyesight to identify conspecifics (turtles of the same species), food, and potential danger. Turtles respond to certain colors. Normally, the colors red, orange, and yellow elicit investigative responses from turtles that are looking for a meal.

Bright, red eyes are a characteristic of male North American box turtles (*Terrapene* spp.). Based upon observations of this species in captivity, the brilliance fades from the male's eyes immediately after mating. This trait suggests that the color of the box turtle's eyes has a hormonal basis. Regardless of the reason behind the brilliant color, it undoubtedly provides a visual signal to females that the male is ready to mate.

Hearing is another sense used by turtles. Although turtles lack an ear opening, a fleshy membrane called the tympanum covers their ears. Within the middle

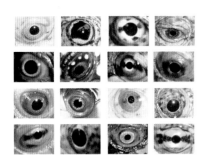

These sixteen eyes represent a fraction of the eyeball diversity among chelonians.

ear, the columnella bone translates airborne vibrations into sound.

Despite the fact that turtles lack vocal chords, many of them can produce sounds. Sound production among turtles is most often the result of air being forced from the lungs. However, various species emit other distinctive sounds. The red-footed tortoise of South America periodically emits a series of clucks, not unlike that of a hen. Mating male Travancore tortoises (*Indotestudo forstenii*) of southeastern Asia are one of many tortoise species that emit a high-pitched whine that is similar to the buzz of a small electric motor. Another turtle known to emit strange noises is the leatherback sea turtle; nesting females sometimes make sounds similar to a human belch.

One specimen of a giant musk turtle (*Staurotypus* sp.) of Central America has been noted for "crying." Coincidentally, the scenario that included the crying of *Staurotypus* took place while the turtle was being slaughtered. I have three large adult specimens of *Staurotypus* in my personal collection. One evening I placed them on my bathroom floor. Later that evening, unusual yelp-like sounds came from the bathroom. It soon became clear that the noises were the result of the turtles startling one another as they bumped into one another in the dark. As I continued listening, the "yelps" sounded more like an exaggerated swallowing sound followed by a hiss of air.

The sense of touch is also important, as it allows turtles to thermoregulate, select ideal refuge sites, detect climatic changes, locate prey, and feel vibrations transmitted across the ground by approaching organisms. Some species, such as the matamata (*Chelus fimbriatus*) of South America, possess fleshy ornamentations on their limbs and necks, and barbels hang from their chins. Both of these physical features can be useful in interpreting and sending tactile cues. The ornamentation of the matamata contains nerve endings that can alert the turtle to the presence of fish in its murky environment. The fleshy chin barbels allow a means for gentle touching along the neck and face during courtship.

While the aforementioned senses are straightforward in their operation, the chemosensory senses operate in a slightly more intimate manner because they rely on receiving and processing chemical signals. The chemical signals are used to interpret information about their surroundings. Smells are invisible and transmissible through substrate materials, water, and air. Male turtles ready to mate often use the sense of smell. To confirm the sex of a potential mate, males sniff the area close to the tail.

Many tortoises have a pair of scent glands just below their chins, while other chelonians have scent glands in the axillary (point of insertion for the front limbs) or inguinal (near the point of insertion of the hind legs) portions of their shells.

Smell is also useful in locating food. By using their well-developed sense of smell, opportunistic turtles spurred on by the scent of a ready meal often locate ripe fruit and carrion. Aside from finding food and mates, the sense of smell can help a turtle avoid potential danger. In a laboratory experiment, common musk turtles behaved normally in their terrarium until water that had been used in a terrarium that housed an alligator snapping turtle was added to their tank. Adding that water caused the turtles to clamber around their tank in an attempt to escape. Subsequent trials indicated that the turtles became alarmed by the chemosensory presence of the predator.

Chapter 2
Ecology

Turtles succeed not only because of their protective shells, but because of their ability to exploit numerous environmental niches. Some species are habitat generalists, such as the red-eared slider (*Trachemys scripta elegans*) and the common snapping turtle (*Chelydra serpentina*). These adaptable species can make a living in rivers, ponds, lakes, or even brackish waters.

The world's oceans and seas cover more than 70 percent of the earth's surface yet provide a habitat for only seven species of turtles. Sea turtles, which have changed very little from their prehistoric ancestors, are the only chelonians adapted for living in a saltwater environment. Long-term exposure to salt water causes physiological problems for most reptiles. Excess amounts of salt in the body of a nonmarine reptile can interfere with basic cellular functions.

A number of freshwater turtles can tolerate brackish water, which forms where an outflowing source of fresh water meets a body of salt water. Vegetation such as mangroves and reeds, cattails, and a variety of grasses characterizes such environments. The diamondback terrapin (*Malaclemys terrapin*) is one species that is well adapted to living in brackish waters.

*Ornate box turtle (*Terrapene ornata*).*
David C. Killpack

David C. Killpack

Many freshwater turtle species engage in mutualistic behavior. In this illustration, a grackle plucks leeches off an Ouachita map turtle (Graptemys ouachitensis), and a school of blacknose dace cleans a North American wood turtle (Glyptemys insculpta). Even the algae covering the shell of a common snapping turtle (Chelydra serpentina) adds to its camouflage, while the turtle's behavior facilitates the growth of the garden of algae.

Although most of the world's water is salty, most turtle species live in or near bodies of fresh water. Ponds, lakes, rivers, rice paddies, creeks, and streams provide the necessary habitat for many aquatic turtle species.

Turtles have also become quite successful at establishing a niche for a terrestrial existence. Land-dwelling species can be found on almost every country that contains turtles (except for Australia and Madagascar). Tortoises represent the highest diversity of chelonians that have adapted well for a life on land. The design of their bodies and survival strategies have allowed them to successfully exploit an array of habitats, ranging from the sandy pine hammocks of Florida to the cool, wet mountainsides in Myanmar to the hot, arid, and seemingly inhospitable Mojave Desert of southern California.

Because of their ability to master the life aquatic and terrestrial, turtles have successfully adapted and evolved into the forms we see today.

Thermoregulation

Like all reptiles, turtles are ectothermic, or cold-blooded. Ectotherms do not generate metabolic body heat from burning calories; instead, the temperature of their surroundings directly influences their body temperature. Not surprisingly, turtle shells play an important role in the thermoregulatory process.

Many species of freshwater turtles openly bask in the sunlight on warm days, which affords spectators a great opportunity to witness turtle behavior. Sometimes there are more turtles than available basking sites. When this problem arises, many turtles (especially aquatic members of the family Emydidae) stack themselves on top of one another in an attempt to receive the sunlight. Often while basking, turtles try to receive as much sunlight as possible by extending their neck and legs.

Most freshwater turtles have dark carapaces that absorb solar heat. When they become too warm, the

*Basking is the most common method turtles use to regulate their body temperature. Seen here is a group of savanna side-necked turtles (*Podocnemis vogli*) vying for prime basking sites.*

turtles slip away from the rays of the sun and lower their body temperature by diving beneath the cool surface of the water.

Basking helps aquatic turtles increase their metabolic rate for food digestion, rid themselves of ectoparasites, and reduce the amount of algae accumulating on their shells. Excessive amounts of algae can reduce a turtle's swimming speed or hinder underwater maneuverability.

While numerous aquatic turtles engage in this behavior, there is one major exception. The leatherback sea turtle rarely, if ever, basks, yet it maintains a stable body temperature even in freezing temperatures. In fact, the core body temperature of an adult leatherback barely fluctuates at all. Leatherbacks are capable of maintaining a constant and relatively high body temperature because of their low metabolic rate, insulation from fat reserves and vascularized cartilage, and a lower surface area to body mass index. This condition is called gigantothermy.

Feeding and Diet

In general, turtles appreciate a wide variety of food types. Most turtles are omnivores and take advantage of whatever suitable meal is available. However, some species possess a specialized digestive system that allows them to exercise a selective dietary intake. These turtles feed almost entirely on a restricted selection of food items. For example, the hawksbill sea turtle (*Eretmochelys imbricata*), which feeds primarily on sponges, has a digestive system capable of breaking down the silica contained within sponges.

The leatherback sea turtle (*Dermochelys coriacea*), which consumes a diet chiefly comprised of jellyfish, possesses a modified cusp and lining inside the mouth and esophagus that is especially adapted for ingesting the gelatinous creatures. Keratinized papillae extend from the inside of the leatherback's mouth into a long esophagus that can measure up to 6.5 feet (2 meters). While feeding, these seafaring behemoths swallow considerable amounts of seawater. The esophageal projections help secure the slippery jellyfish within the digestive system when water is expelled.

Adult female North American map turtles (*Graptemys* spp.) prey heavily on mussels. These turtles experience an ontogenetic development in head size from juvenile to adult. The dramatic increase in the width and thickness of the turtle's head, called macrocephaly, is proportionate to the gain of muscle mass and the crushing power necessary to consume hard-shelled mollusks. The same condition occurs among several other species of Australian turtles (*Chelodina*, *Elseya*, *Emydura*, and *Macrochelodina*). Sometimes the degree of macrocephaly found in Australian snake-necked turtles is so extensive that they have difficulty lifting their heads when out of the water.

The majority of terrestrial turtles are herbivores, while most aquatic species prefer a carnivorous diet.

*Whether consuming grasses, leaves, fruits, or vegetables, herbivorous turtles such as these Galápagos tortoises (*Geochelone nigra*) use their cusps to slice and cut their food into easy-to-swallow pieces.*

*The keeled box turtle (*Pyxidea mouhotii*) sometimes uses its front feet to bring food to its mouth.*

However, there do not seem to be absolutes regarding herbivory or carnivory. For example, the soft-shelled turtles of the family Trionychidae are largely predators, but some species of this family occasionally eat aquatic vegetation.

Tortoises represent the one family of turtles that is almost solely herbivorous. With their well-developed visual acuity, tortoises are successful at selecting the most delectable of plants, grasses, leaves, fruits, and vegetables. Their cusps cut vegetation like pruning shears. However, not all tortoises are strict vegetarians. Red-footed tortoises (*Geochelone carbonaria*) and certain populations of leopard tortoises (*Geochelone pardalis*) sometimes consume animal protein in the form of carrion.

Most turtles eat by holding the food in place with their front feet while biting off pieces. However, the keeled box turtle (*Pyxidea mouhotii*) sometimes carries food to its mouth with its front feet.

In the eastern United States, the alligator snapping turtle (*Macrochelys temminckii*) lures fish to swim into its gaping mouth. While remaining motionless with its mouth wide open, the alligator snapping turtle wriggles a bright pink tongue. The

*The bright fleshy tongue of this alligator snapping turtle (*Macrochelys temminckii*) is the last thing seen by some fish. Offset by the drab coloration inside the mouth, the tongue resembles a tempting worm.*

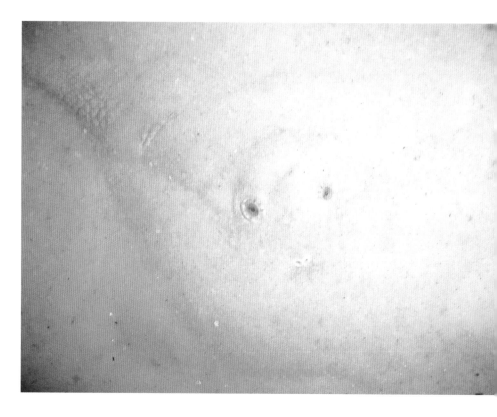

Sometimes waiting for a meal to venture within reach is easier than foraging and hunting. The eyes are the only visible cue that a hungry Cantor's giant soft-shelled turtle (Pelochelys cantori) is waiting beneath the sand.

undulating tongue resembles the final twitches of a drowning earthworm. Once a curious fish ventures too close, the mouth slams shut, and the fish is never seen again.

When a fish ventures too close to the mouth of a matamata (*Chelus fimbriatus*), it is instantly inhaled. This South American species of the family Chelidae employs a prey capture method reminiscent of a largemouth bass. The jawbones of the matamata are thin and relatively weak. To capture prey, the matamata opens its large mouth rapidly, while the throat expands and increases in girth. This movement creates a negative pressure and the prey item, along with water, fills the throat. Muscular movements along the throat and the limited opening of the mouth permit the expulsion of water while preventing the turtle's meal from escaping.

Aside from their ambush suction method of feeding, captive matamatas occasionally hunt their prey. During experimental trials, researchers at the Beardsley Zoological Garden in New York learned that matamatas that are familiar with their setting occasionally trap groups of fish by herding them into restricted locations.

Other South American turtles that use suction to obtain food include river turtles of the family Podocnemidae. Aside from foraging for ripe fruits that fall into the water, these turtles also use a feeding method known as neustophagia. This method involves sucking floating particulate matter into the mouth, swallowing the food matter, and expelling water through the nostrils. This mode of feeding contributes significantly to the diet of turtles living in an environment that has abundant mosquito larvae.

The most interesting technique used by a turtle to acquire food is "worm stomping." This behavior is exhibited by certain populations of the North American wood turtle (*Glyptemys insculpta*), which stomp their feet and drop their plastrons repeatedly against the ground. The result is that earthworms surface and provide a ready meal for the hungry turtles.

Turtles and tortoises play a significant role in the ecology of various plant species. Not only do they eat numerous insects that feed on plants, but they also serve as inadvertent seed dispersers. The seeds of most plants are not susceptible to a turtle's digestive system, so they pass undamaged with the turtle's feces.

For turtles inhabiting fresh water or locations that receive sufficient rainfall, obtaining plenty of water from the environment or from food items is rather easy. However, specializations are necessary for species that live in salt water or in arid climates.

The South African star tortoises (*Psammobates* spp.) and Home's hinge-back tortoises (*Kinixys homeana*) of west-central Africa use their shells to channel rainwater toward the mouth. These tortoises are equipped with shells that have furrows between the scutes of the carapace. When drops of rain land on the shell, the tortoise raises its hind legs and extends its forelimbs alongside its outstretched neck to its head. The water flows off the shell, down the legs, and into its waiting mouth.

The desert tortoise (*Gopherus agassizii*) excavates furrows in the ground to catch rainwater. Upon the arrival of rain, these furrows provide the thirsty tortoise with a long drink.

For sea turtles as well as diamondback terrapins, the salty habitat requires special physical adaptations. These turtles possess salt excretion glands near the corner of the eye. The glands are the reason that nesting female sea turtles appear to be crying while on land. A closer inspection reveals that this clear substance is gooey, thick, and highly concentrated

with salt. Although the substance is salty, it has nothing to do with maternal emotion; it is merely a means for the body to rid itself of excess salt.

Courtship and Reproduction

Vision and olfactory cues are important for turtles seeking a potential mate. Males of many species indicate their readiness to mate by displaying bright colors. Male painted terrapins (*Callagur borneoensis*) of Southeast Asia indicate their readiness to mate with a dramatic change in body coloration. For most of the year, these turtles are gray in overall coloration. They have a series of three broken dark lines and a dark spot on each of the marginal scutes. An orange spot on top of the head is the only bright color that offsets an otherwise drab color scheme. During the breeding season, the gray areas of the body lighten. The carapace brightens in tone and changes to a creamy white or tan. The skin on the upper, or dorsal, surfaces

Matt Vaughn

*No other species of turtle undergoes as much of a dramatic color change as the painted terrapin (*Callagur borneoensis*). This coloration lasts only during the breeding season, after which males revert back to their original drab grayish brown coloration.*

of the head and neck also changes to white, and the orange spot on the head turns a brilliant crimson. After undergoing the color change, the head retains some of the dark pigment around the edges of the eyes, around the sides of the red spot, and on the cusp. The chromatic shift serves as a strong visual signal to females that the male is ready to mate.

While visual cues work well for terrestrial turtles seeking mates, imagine living in an environment where vision is not always possible. Such is life in the sometimes-murky underwater realm of aquatic turtles. Mud and musk turtles that belong to the family Kinosternidae live in such places. When searching for females, the males rely heavily upon scent. Even in a well-lit aquarium that contains clear water, a male still approaches the female from behind after following his nose.

Like other vertebrates, courtship among turtles preludes mating. Depending on species, health, and age, chelonian courtships run the gamut from intricately arranged appeasements that ultimately lead to the seduction of the female to those that are brutal and direct in their intent.

Members of the family Emydidae engage in an aquatic courtship in which the much smaller male orients himself directly in front of the female. With his palms pointed outward, he uses his elongated claws to rapidly stroke and move the water next to the female's tympanum, face, and neck. After performing this exercise for some time, the male attempts to mount the female from behind. If she is not willing to copulate (and does not leave), the male may begin his courtship anew, attempt to mate despite her unwillingness, simply give up, or try again later.

The mating behavior of some tortoises begins with rough bouts of combat. The males of many tortoise species develop elongated scales on the throat called gular scutes. Males use these projecting scutes for combat during the mating season. The gular scutes serve as battering rams as well as levers that are capable of overturning rivals. In parts of southern Texas, the clacking noise caused by combating male Berlandier's tortoises (*Gopherus berlandieri*) ramming their shells is heard from spring to early summer. Sometimes the male uses these projections while trying to subdue the female into mating. During such coercions, the male typically corners the female and rams her side until she submits to his intentions.

Other tortoises demonstrate a gentle nature in their courtship methods. Instead of using brute force and offensive behavior, some males utilize the

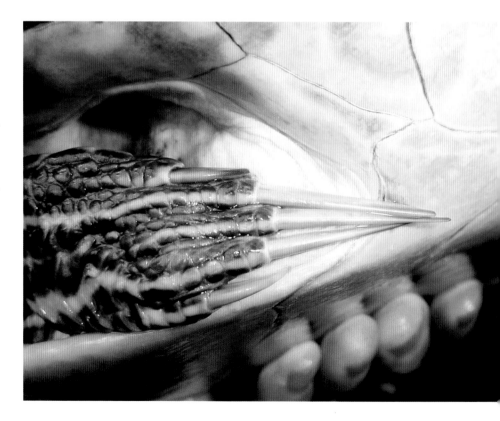

*The elongated claws on the feet of this male river cooter (*Pseudemys concinna*) of the eastern United States are used when courting females. The male places these next to either side of the female's head and vibrates the water with rapid movements of his wrist.*

courtship method of standing directly in front of the female while swaying and bobbing their head.

A number of factors influence when chelonians reproduce. Each species is different and sexual maturity occurs at different ages. Some aquatic turtles, as well as leatherback sea turtles, are capable of reproduction as young as three to five years of age. Terrestrial species, such as the North American wood turtle (*Glyptemys insculpta*), achieve sexual maturity at ten to fifteen years. Sea turtles of the family Cheloniidae require around thirty years before they mature.

As a general rule of thumb, terrestrial turtles mate on land while aquatic species mate in the water. For aquatic turtles, mating in or under the water normally presents no risk for the females. However, there have been incidents where overly enthusiastic males accidentally drowned their mates.

When it comes to laying eggs, two species of turtle prefer to nest where the eggs can get wet. The Central American river turtle (*Dermatemys mawii*) is so aquatic that it maneuvers poorly out of the water and rarely ventures onto land. Females select nest locations close to the water. In fact, the nest is often so close to the water that the eggs submerge as water levels increase from bouts of rainfall. Fortunately, embryonic *Dermatemys* are capable of tolerating full submersion during the early stages of development. Studies have revealed that the embryos can tolerate up to twenty-eight days underwater. After the water levels subside, the eggs hatch and the young turtles leave their nest.

Northern Australian snake-necked turtles (*Macrochelodina rugosa*) of the billabongs and lagoons of northern Australia and southern New Guinea lay their eggs in an underwater nest. The females seek shallow locations for their nest sites. The eggs remain in the aquatic nest until the arrival of the dry season. Hatching commences after water levels drop and air reaches the eggs. The only catch, of course, is that after the body of water has dried, the baby turtles are trapped underground and must wait until the following year when the rains return to soften the hard, baked earth. Until then, the little turtles remain prisoners beneath the ground.

When a female turtle chooses a location for her nest, she selects an area that seems ideal for maintaining the environmental needs of her eggs. Temperature and humidity play a crucial role in the development of embryonic turtles.

*This female three-toed box turtle (*Terrapene carolina triunguis*) has just deposited her eggs into the nest. Like the females of many other species, she laid her eggs at night under the cover of darkness.*

Many female turtles travel great distances to find an ideal nesting location. Female common snapping turtles (*Chelydra serpentina*) sometimes travel more than 2 miles (5 kilometers) across land to lay their eggs. However, sea turtles by far out-rival all other species. Leatherback sea turtles have traveled up to 7,456 miles (12,000 kilometers) to their nesting beaches.

The surface of a turtle egg is semipermeable, which allows an exchange of respired gasses to take place. As the embryo grows and metabolic activities take place, the egg absorbs oxygen and releases carbon dioxide. Just the right amount of moisture prevents the egg from desiccating, yet too much moisture can ruin the egg or possibly drown the embryo.

*Staring at the world for the first time, this recently hatched red-footed tortoise (*Geochelone carbonaria*) from a captive breeding program in Venezuela will require up to a week to completely absorb its yolk sac. In the wild, hatchling turtles wait until the yolk is absorbed before leaving the egg.*

In most organisms, including humans, chromosomes determine the sex of an embryo. For a handful of turtle species, including giant musk turtles, the sex of unhatched offspring is indeed determined chromosomally. However, for most turtle species—and all crocodilian and some lizard species—temperature determines the sex of embryos as well as the rate of incubation. Each species of turtle that relies upon temperature-dependent sexual determination has its own unique range of temperatures that dictate the sex of the embryo.

For the most part, turtle eggs are highly vulnerable. Fortunately, females employ a few strategies to enhance the survival of the developing turtles. Prior to depositing their eggs, some females such as North American box turtles and numerous species of pond turtles dig more than one nest hole. This behavior likely results from a female trying to select the most suitable location for her eggs. However, the remaining vacant nest sites potentially sidetrack hungry predators.

Leaving multiple vacant nests is a passive defense ploy at best. Two species of turtles play a more active role in defending their progeny. The female Asian brown tortoise (*Manouria emys*) that inhabits the montane forests of Southeast Asia constructs a mound of dead leaves and vegetation that can measure 2 feet

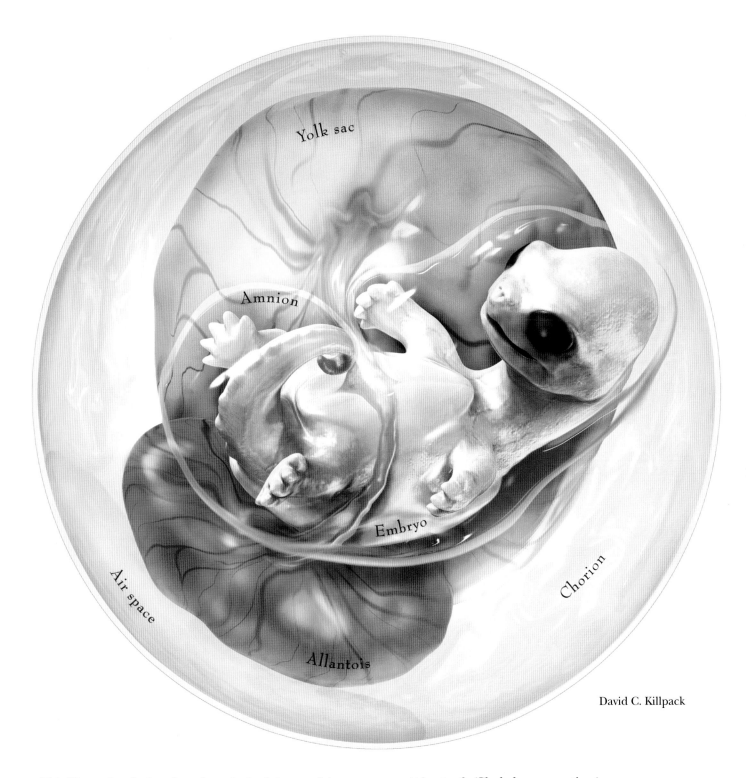

*This illustration depicts the embryonic development of the common snapping turtle (*Chelydra serpentina*).*

David C. Killpack

Witnessing a turtle hatching in the wild is not a common event. However, many hatchings have been observed in captive populations. Pictured here are two endangered species hatching from their eggs: the Annam leaf turtle (Mauremys annamensis) *and the common spider tortoise* (Pyxis arachnoides).

(60 centimeters) high and more than 5 feet (1.5 meters) in diameter. Following construction, the female excavates a cavity within the mound and deposits her eggs. After laying the eggs, she promptly sits on top of the mound. From this vantage point, the female watches for potential predators. Tortoises are rather slow, and the Asian brown tortoise is no exception. Essentially, the tortoise defends her eggs by lying directly on top of them. If a predator attempts to dig into the mound, the female covers that spot with her body. She may even resort to pushing the intruder away. The female guards the nest for a few days and then leaves. By that time, the mound is flattened and resembles the surrounding forest leaf litter.

The yellow mud turtle (*Kinosternon flavescens*) of North America also exhibits nest-guarding behavior. After laying her eggs, the female spends up to two weeks near the nest.

Apart from these exceptions, the females of most turtle species do not tend their nests and will leave their eggs the moment that they are covered.

The intrinsic toughness of a turtle's egg should not be discounted as a survival factor. Caveats of natural selection often play roles that challenge the imagination. A kingsnake found at the Savannah River Plant in South Carolina regurgitated four hard-shelled turtle eggs shortly after capture. Three days later, the snake defecated thirteen turtle eggs, three of which were unbroken. The three unbroken eggs were placed in an incubator for fifty days, whereupon three healthy common musk turtles (*Sternotherus odoratus*) hatched. Amazingly, the powerful digestive enzymes in the snake's stomach had no effect on the eggs!

Before and after hatching, baby turtles do not exactly have the odds in their favor. Invariably, some of the eggs never hatch successfully. Fortunately, the presence of turtles today indicates that there are plenty of exceptions.

Predators

From the moment the female lays her eggs until the turtles hatch and reach maturity, chelonians are at risk of predation before they can reproduce. Fortunately, millions of years of evolution have given them the means to cope with some of these pressures.

Predatory invertebrates normally prey upon other invertebrates. Nevertheless, their predatory instincts command them to hunt, capture, and consume any appropriately sized prey. In the southeastern United States, the notoriously invasive fire ant is causing more problems than mere blistering stings. The ants enter nests and destroy turtle eggs that have slight imperfections. The ants also kill the turtles as they cut through their eggshells during hatching. Fire ants are not native to the United States, and they pose a significant threat to turtles and their eggs.

In 2000, a biologist at a nature center in Fort Worth, Texas, scooped a random sample of water from the Trinity River and added it to an aquarium for a teaching display. The water contained aquatic plants and several active aquatic invertebrates. After the detritus had settled and the visibility improved, the biologist noticed a large, predaceous aquatic beetle. A closer inspection revealed that the beetle had captured and was consuming a hatchling common musk turtle (*Sternotherus odoratus*). Crabs can be a significant predator of sea turtle eggs and hatchlings by getting to the eggs before the female covers her nest and then snatching the hatchlings as they leave the nest.

Given the opportunistic nature of predatory invertebrates, it is likely that large centipedes, scorpions, and spiders occasionally capture and consume small turtles. While species from all classes of vertebrates opportunistically prey upon turtles, none are specialized for hunting them exclusively.

Predatory freshwater fish—including gar, catfish, and bass in North America and numerous other fish around the world—prey upon turtles. Various species of saltwater fish take newly hatched sea turtles, while sharks pose the only significant threat to adults. On land, tiger salamanders, mature bullfrogs, and large toads represent some of the amphibious predators that are willing to eat virtually any suitably sized prey. Many reptiles prey upon turtles. Adult snapping turtles (family Chelydridae) and giant musk turtles (*Staurotypus* spp.) sometimes eat smaller turtles, such as the musk turtles of the family Kinosternidae.

As with bird eggs, many snakes actively seek and prey upon turtle eggs. A king snake in Florida was observed discreetly approaching a female gopher tortoise that was laying her eggs. As the tortoise deposited her eggs, the king snake stealthily consumed a few as they left the female. Another North American snake that has demonstrated a fondness for turtle eggs is the bull snake. These powerful constrictors have been documented consuming the recently laid eggs of ornate box turtles (*Terrapene ornata*).

A hole drilled in the turtle's carapace allows indigenous people to tether the animal until it is time to be eaten.

Eric N. Smith

A cord is sewn between the carapace and plastron of this live soft-shelled turtle. The cord keeps the front of shell closed, preventing the animal from biting, while also providing a handle for the purchaser to carry the turtle.

The enthusiasm for eggs demonstrated by monitor lizards is also well established. Like snakes, monitor lizards utilize a sensitive forked tongue to interpret biochemical cues. A highly evolved sense of smell, combined with claws capable of digging, make monitor lizards a formidable predator of turtle eggs.

Danger for turtles also comes from the sky. Grackles, crows, egrets, gulls, frigates, wading birds, and raptors occasionally find hatchlings or other suitably sized individuals and pluck them from the ground or water. Some hawks have demonstrated an interesting strategy for making the most of a chelonian meal. In central Asia, golden eagles fly away with a tortoise in their talons and drop it onto large rocks. The impact from the fall is often enough to break the shell open and expose the meat inside. Should the first attempt prove ineffective, the eagle retrieves the tortoise and ascends to greater heights in order to repeat the procedure.

Almost all carnivorous mammals have some record of preying upon turtles. Raccoons, coati mundi, opossums, skunks, dogs, coyotes, dingo, foxes, jackals, feral hogs, and wolves are just some of the mammals that eat eggs, hatchlings, and adult turtles. Domestic and wild cats take advantage of suitably sized turtles. Tortoises in Africa and South America have been found with indentations in their shells from the teeth of a lion or jaguar. Pumas, jaguars, and wild dogs exploit the vulnerability of nesting sea turtles.

This juvenile specimen of South American river turtle (Podocnemis expansa) *was offered for sale for food in Iquitos, Peru.*

Despite the number of eggs and turtles eaten by predatory mammals, humans consume more turtles than any other vertebrate predators. Today's Chinese food trade constitutes the largest volume of turtles consumed by humans. Many of China's turtle populations have long since been depleted, resulting in the demand for imports from other countries. According to one researcher, more than 12 million turtles are sold each year in China alone! Sadly, this trend is continuing and shows no sign of slowing down.

The turtle diversity of several nations—including Bangladesh, Pakistan, India, Nepal, Papua New Guinea, the United States, and Vietnam—have all been affected by the indiscriminate removal of turtles from the wild. In fact, the number of turtles imported to China from other nations has increased tenfold since 1977. Exporting an estimated 1.84 to 18 tons of turtles daily, Vietnam is the largest supplier of turtles to China. While some dead specimens are used in medicinal practices, live specimens represent a majority of turtles sent to the Chinese food markets.

To exacerbate the situation, many species found in the markets are listed as protected under international law. It is not uncommon to find specimens listed under the Convention of International Trade of Endangered Species Act (CITES). The current trend of making a profit from turtles reflects a flagrant disregard for laws specifically designed to protect wildlife from such exploitation. At least some of the one ton of turtles exported to China from the United States each week avoids U.S. Fish and Wildlife Service (USFWS) scrutiny by bearing the label "Seafood."

Given the current trends of the Chinese turtle trade, most of the world's turtle populations are vulnerable to becoming severely depleted or extinct. Already two species are believed to be extinct due to the trade. Ironically, both of these

Matt Vaughn

*The cryptic coloration of the matamata (*Chelus fimbriatus*) allows it to patrol muddy creeks in the Peruvian Amazon without attracting the attention of visually oriented predators.*

species were originally discovered at a Chinese marketplace. McCord's box turtle (*Cuora mccordi*) was first described to the scientific community in 1988, and Zhou's box turtle (*Cuora zhoui*) was described in 1990. Shortly following their description, neither of these species has ever been seen again, despite the offer of a significant bounty. Only awareness will stem the tide of turtle exploitation. Only by educating people about the important role turtles and other living things play in the balance of life can we hope to cause a cultural shift.

Defense Strategies

Turtles would not have survived for hundreds of millions of years without the ability to defend or protect themselves from danger. The most commonly utilized form of chelonian self-defense is leaving a potentially dangerous situation. Escape is often a viable option for basking aquatic turtles. In most situations, the slightest disturbance will cause a carefully arranged pile of basking turtles to clamber all at once into the water. Startled soft-shelled turtles often dive into the water, bury themselves beneath the detritus, and wait for some time before they surface. Sliders (*Trachemys* spp.) and cooters (*Pseudemys* spp.) dive and remain briefly submerged before cautiously raising their heads to take a breath of air and survey the situation.

Many species of freshwater and terrestrial turtles rely on the ability to go about their affairs unnoticed. Cryptic colorations that camouflage are especially important for species dwelling on land. Some terrestrial turtles, such as the common box turtle (*Terrapene carolina*), display bold and colorful hues. This may seem as counterintuitive for camouflage, but these colors and patterns effectively conceal the turtles in a forest habitat where sunlight is dappled by the canopy before it reaches the ground.

Most chelonians that use camouflage take a more orthodox approach for going unnoticed. Leopard tortoises (*Geochelone pardalis*) bear subdued tones of creamy yellow, brown, beige, and black that help them go about their affairs unnoticed in the grasslands of Africa.

Some freshwater turtles benefit from an accumulation of algal growth on their shells. Algae-covered musk turtles (family Kinosternidae) foraging along the bottom of a water body can resemble rocks. Some aquatic turtles are perfectly suited for cryptic concealment within their environment. Alligator snapping turtles (*Macrochelys temminckii*) and matamatas (*Chelus fimbriatus*) both depend on going unnoticed to catch unwary fish. In the case of the alligator snapping turtle, the grayish-brown ridged shell covered with juxtaposed scutes could easily pass as an inanimate object. The crypsis in the alligator snapping turtles does not end there. Smattered shades of gray and brown that resemble patches of mud line the inside of the mouth. The only part of the alligator snapping turtle's appearance that is not cryptic is the tongue, which is bright pink and offsets the drab, mud-like coloration inside the mouth. To potential prey, the tongue is nothing more than a drowning earthworm that is twitching away its last amount of energy.

When threatened, a number of turtles and tortoises urinate, defecate, or emit a pungent, foul-smelling odor. Urination and defecation may simply be an artifact of any frightened creature that is captured or picked up by another. However, potential predators are likely to find the taste of fecal matter or urine repugnant and then decide to eat something else.

More investigations are necessary to gain a better understanding of how effective it is for turtles to emit a foul smell as a defense ploy. However, observations support the notion that a stinky turtle is a safe turtle. Australian turtle expert John Cann observed catfish gulping down recently hatched snake-necked turtles, only to promptly expel them. After the catfish spit them out, the little turtles remained motionless on their backs, displaying their bright orange-red plastrons. Snake-necked turtle hatchlings emit a foul-smelling substance when handled. Although I have not tasted this substance to verify my claim, the chemical responsible for the odor likely tastes terrible.

Displays of bright colors, called aposematic coloration, warn predators of a potentially distasteful or poisonous meal. The snake-necked hatchlings were likely displaying their brightly colored plastrons as an aposematic warning to the catfish. A few incidents of human poisoning have even been associated with the consumption of common box turtles (*Terrapene carolina*). Box turtles consume a variety of mushrooms, including poisonous species, and the instances of human poisoning were likely due to toxins stored after the turtles consumed poisonous mushrooms.

Box turtles that have just left the nest chamber often discharge a foul-smelling liquid when handled for the first time. However, their capacity to produce

Sometimes a good defense equals a good offense. The thick and powerful jaws of the Mexican giant musk turtle (Staurotypus triporcatus) *have incredible strength and are capable of inflicting serious injury.*

the substance quickly diminishes. The liquid is likely a result of the body storing urine for extended amounts of time while the turtles were encased within the nest chamber. Since the shells of newly hatched turtles are thin, inhibiting the release of urine could significantly prevent desiccation.

As suggested by their name, the musk turtles of the family Kinosternidae can emit a foul-smelling, pungent odor. The common musk turtle (*Sternotherus odoratus*) is so renowned for its ability that it also has the nickname "stinkpot turtle."

Aggressive behavior is not normally associated with a frightened turtle. Given their evolutionary design and inclination to withdraw from threats, the irony of an aggressive turtle is obvious. What humans see as aggression among many animals is often misinterpreted behavior.

Take, for instance, the following account from 1905 involving a 610-pound (280-kilogram) loggerhead sea turtle (*Caretta caretta*). The text is from an article that appeared in the *New York Tribune*. Undoubtedly stirring some excitement among readers, the headline boldly proclaimed "Big turtle victor over five men: Loggerhead which figured in cruelty to animals case resist efforts to recapture it."

South Norwalk, Conn., Saturday.—Five East Norwalk fishermen crawled into port last evening using the stumps of their oars as paddles and with one of their number unconscious in the bottom of the boat as the result to attempt to catch the famous 610-pound loggerhead turtle which escaped from Captain Charles E. Ducross, a south Norwalk market man, and which was the largest and most vicious turtle of this species ever brought into Fulton Market.

This is the turtle whose flippers were pierced by Captain Ducross and the owner arrested and fined for animal cruelty to animals. The Captain was found guilty and fined $5 and cost at a time when the turtle had escaped from his pen. The mammoth chelonian tore down and crunched the planks on the side of the pen as though they were toothpicks.

Captain Ducross offered a reward of $50 for the recapture of the turtle, and Frank Petty with his two sons, Frank and George, and two other men named Swanson set out yesterday morning in a rowboat intending to catch the chelonian. They took nets and spears and rope aplenty.

The Petty party found the turtle asleep in the harbor, not far from where it had been seen the afternoon before by the captain of the Oyster Steamer Josephine. They approached him slowly and cautiously. Swanson, who is an expert fisherman and sailor, attempted to drive an eel spear, to which a long and heavy line was attached, through the back of the turtle. The spear broke off short in the tough shell of the turtle and then there commenced a fight which lasted nearly an hour.

The chelonian seemed to have no fear of the men or the boat. He turned upon them and with his flippers almost overturned the boat. The five men beat him over the head with the oars. These he occasionally got in his mouth and each in turn was crunched and broken off. It was in the thickest of the fight that Swanson was struck by either one of the flippers of the animal or the beak and a long gash was torn in his arm. In spite of the wound Swanson assisted with the fight until the turtle withdrew and sank out of sight, apparently none the worse for his encounter.

It took the party nearly two hours to paddle their craft, which was nearly full of water, back to this port. They all say they do not intend to try to capture any more loggerheads, reward or no reward, and that Judge Taylor, who fined Captain Ducross for piercing the turtle's flippers, ought to be fined for not instructing the owner to cut off its head for the general welfare.

Based on the sentiments from the men involved in the conflict, most readers would believe that the turtle was actively attacking the men and their boat. However, one must consider that the sleeping turtle was jolted from sleep and startled from being speared, and the men were actively making every attempt to capture and subdue the animal. Given such, it is of little wonder that the turtle became aggressive toward the five men in the boat!

In the water, common snapping turtles (*Chelydra serpentina*) and alligator snapping turtles (*Macrochelys temminckii*) can deliver powerful bites and inflict serious injury. While fishing in the Brazos River near Marlin, Texas, during the 1940s, my great uncle lost his big toe after he carelessly stepped too close to a large snapping turtle. On land, a threatened snapping turtle raises its body and rapidly lunges its snapping mouth at anyone foolish enough to molest it. When picked up, giant musk turtles (*Staurotypus* spp.) open their mouths wide and present the prospect of a painful lesson. Likewise, most species of soft-shelled turtles kick, scrape with their claws, and rapidly lunge their heads in an attempt to bite anyone who attempts to capture or restrain them.

Seasonal Periods of Inactivity

Occasionally, turtles reduce or cease their body's normal metabolic activities. Climatic changes influence such periods of dormancy. During hot and dry summer months, turtles avoid overheating by seeking a cool and humid retreat where they can essentially shut down their bodily functions. This cessation of summer activity is called aestivation. Before aestivating during times of drought and intense heat, some aquatic turtles attempt an overland migration to locate better bodies of water. Terrestrial turtles must rely on the familiarity of their home range to select ideal refuge sites. In eastern Arizona, the desert box turtle (*Terrapene ornata luteola*) sometimes seeks relief from the heat by burrowing into moist cowpies. The spur-thighed tortoise (*Testudo graeca*) of sub-Saharan Africa prevents overheating by excavating deep tunnels that can measure more than 20 feet (6 meters) in length. These underground retreats provide a cool refuge from the blazing equatorial sun. Even in the wet tropical rainforests of Malaysia, the keeled box turtle (*Pyxidea mouhotii*) remains inactive beneath moist piles of leaf litter until the return of the rainy season.

Aestivation not only protects turtles from overheating and depleting resources necessary for metabolic functions, it also helps them survive natural disasters. From time to time, various species of terrestrial turtles are found with fire-scarred shells. In several places throughout the world, forest or grassland fires are an annual event promoted by dry seasons and often ignited by lightning. Other times, the spark of a wildfire comes from carelessly discarded cigarettes or intentional land clearings. Wildfires occur most often during the peak of the dry season and the terrestrial turtles are already aestivating. The refuge site a turtle has chosen for aestivating influences how the intense heat of a wildfire affects the shelled reptile.

Once while collecting reptiles and amphibians in eastern Honduras, I received an interesting brown wood turtle (*Rhinoclemmys annulata*). Upon initially examining the turtle, I could see that fire had melted and even scorched the carapace to the bone. However, it was not until the turtle was calm enough to extend its neck that I could see the full extent of the damage. The fire had burned and damaged the forelimbs and completely scorched away the nose and the soft tissue of the face.

*These red-eared sliders (*Trachemys scripta elegans*) were found walking alongside a dirt road in north Texas at least 1 mile (1.6 kilometers) from the nearest source of permanent water.*

Aquatic turtles inhabiting bodies of water that experience seasonal fluctuations in water levels sometimes burrow into the moist soil or shoreline vegetation to prevent dehydration. Then the turtles remain there until the return of a favorable climate. In Australia, various chelid turtles embark on an overland search for water or bury into the mud until the rains return and replenish the water levels. However, turtles become more vulnerable to humans during this period of dormancy. For example, aboriginal hunters, using their keen sense of environmental awareness, can find the air holes of the buried turtles.

At the onset of winter, turtles and tortoises that inhabit temperate zones prepare for another form of inactivity known as hibernation. Lower temperatures not only limit the activity of turtles but cause

*The trail of a common snapping turtle (*Chelydra serpentina*) leads more than a mile from this rapidly drying pool to a better water body.*

the animals and plants that turtles feed on to become scarce as well. Even if food were available during this time, there would be no way for the turtles to digest the meal without the heat required to promote the necessary metabolic functions.

In temperate zones, loggerhead sea turtles (*Caretta caretta*) sometimes lie dormant in the mud at the bottom of harbors and bays during cold months. The reduction of physiological functions such as heart rate is so significant among some aquatic species that they remain underwater and buried in mud for months at a time. The painted turtle (*Chrysemys picta*) of North America is well suited for handling temperatures that plunge below

freezing. The blood of this species contains chemicals that act essentially as antifreeze, which allows the turtles to survive winters at subfreezing temperatures. When frozen, the blood of most vertebrates forms crystals that pierce and damage the surrounding tissue and typically cause a fatal outcome. In contrast, painted turtles are not only resilient against the cold, but they have even been seen swimming beneath sheets of ice on frozen ponds.

Age

Turtles are long-lived creatures that have the potential to reach ages far exceeding the natural lifespan of humans. The oldest documented chelonian alive in recent times was a Galápagos tortoise (*Geochelone nigra*) collected by Charles Darwin during an 1835 visit to Santa Cruz Island. At that time, the young tortoise was the size of a dinner plate and estimated to be five years old. Until her death in 2006, the 330-pound (150-kilogram) specimen named Harriet was on display at the Australia Zoo in Brisbane, Australia. Harriet was at least 176 years old at the time of her death

The alligator snapping turtle (*Macrochelys temminckii*) is another long-lived species. One specimen captured and slaughtered during the late 1970s had arrowheads and musket balls embedded in its carapace, which dated the turtle back to the 1700s. Another specimen had a carapace containing an embedded .050 caliber shell used exclusively during the Civil War, more than one hundred years past. Considering these accounts, one can imagine that some turtles are capable of living more than two hundred years and may even approach three hundred years of age.

Not all centenarian turtles are large species. In 1921, John Treadwell Nichols, a curator at the American Museum of Natural History, marked several eastern box turtles (*Terrapene carolina carolina*) and released them at the Fire Island National Seashore on the mainland of Long Island, New York. In 2002, during a faunal survey of the area, park officials found a box turtle with the markings JN21-21 near the location where Nichols had released the turtle some eighty years earlier. Nichol's records revealed that JN21-21 was estimated to have been 20 years old at the time of marking, making the turtle 101 years old at the time of recapture!

Despite the accounts of exceptionally long-lived specimens, most turtles do not reach such golden years. For many in the wild, the lifespan is much shorter.

Determining the age of a turtle is tricky. Each year, turtles develop new scutes that form beneath the previous year's growth. The growth results in ring-like markings called annuli, which makes it possible to estimate the turtle's age. Much like rings on a tree, wider spaces between scutes indicate periods of rapid growth. However, counting annuli is an inexact science. Some individuals develop multiple annuli each year and many older specimens have shells worn smooth with age—both reasons why age determination in most chelonians is an estimate at best.

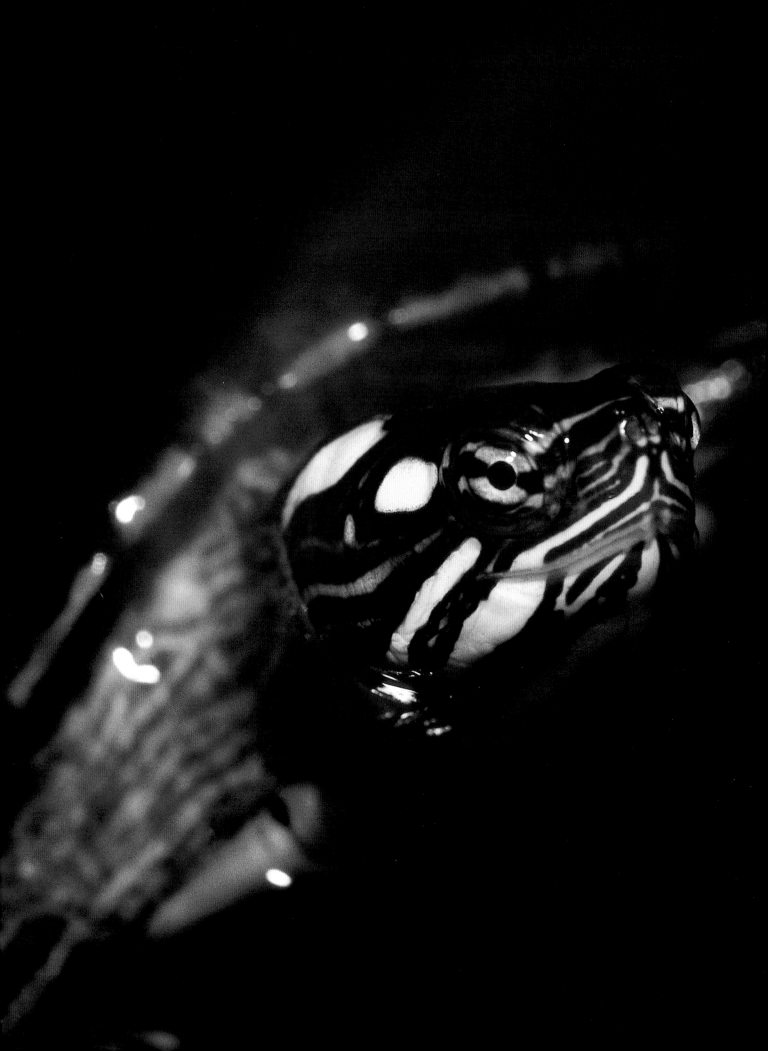

Chapter 3
The Ancient Origins of Turtles

At the end of the Paleozoic era some 280 million years ago, major geologic events caused a dramatic rearrangement of the continents. This rearrangement resulted in changing sea levels and the issuing of a warmer climate. Incredibly, this era bore witness to the extinction of approximately 90 percent of the world's biodiversity.

The Paleozoic era provided the testing grounds for a new type of vertebrate, the amniote. Amniotes are a specialized group of animals that complete their embryonic stages while contained within a sac filled with amniotic fluid. This significant evolutionary step was the key toward animals fully exploiting an existence on dry land. Amniotes include familiar vertebrates such as reptiles, birds, and mammals.

The following era, the Mesozoic, hosted a greater invasion of life onto land than the previous era and set the stage for Earth's next major geologic event. The Mesozoic era includes three distinct periods: the Triassic (245 million to 210 million years ago), the Jurassic (210 million to 144 million years ago), and the Cretaceous (144 million to 65 million years ago). The sheets of ice that had affected global temperatures and sea levels during the Paleozoic melted, and many species of animals moved beyond the equatorial regions to which they were previously restricted.

Northern populations of painted turtles (Chrysemys picta) *are adapted for surviving freezing temperatures. A special chemical in their blood acts as antifreeze.*

The hot, tropical climate that dominated the Triassic period greatly facilitated the evolution of life on land. Dinosaurs appeared and forms of plants that we recognize today arose. It was during these ancient beginnings that a shelled reptile with a familiar form came to be.

The first creature positively identifiable as a turtle made its initial appearance some 245 million years ago during the Triassic period. At least two species represented early turtles: *Proganochelys dux* and *Proganochelys quenstedti.*

Proganochelys was a large turtle that attained lengths up to 2 feet (60 centimeters). While this early chelonian bore many similarities to the turtles of today, there were notable differences. *Proganochelys* could not withdraw its neck or head into its shell, nor did it fold its neck to the side of its body. Instead, a series of armored plates and spines bedecked the long neck. The tail was too long to withdraw into the shell. However, it brandished a well-developed series of armored plates and spines, as well as a clubbed end. Like modern turtles, *Proganochelys* had a toothless cusp, but it also had a series of flattened teeth on the roof of its mouth.

Proganochelys fossil deposits have been recovered in Germany, Greenland, Southeast Asia, and North America. The ecology of this turtle is uncertain. However, due to the other types of fossils associated with those of *Proganochelys*, scientists conclude that this turtle lived near bodies of fresh water.

Jurassic Chelonians

The next major period of the Mesozoic era was the Jurassic, and with it came an increase of chelonian diversity. The remains of the oldest pleurodires, or side-necked turtles, date to the middle of the Jurassic period some 210 million years ago. *Notoemys laticentralis* and *Platychelys oberndorferi* are two species of pleurodirian turtles from this time. Like modern-day side-necked turtles, they appear to have been well-suited to an aquatic lifestyle and capable of folding their heads alongside the front of their shells.

The Jurassic provided the stage for chelonian evolution. During this time, several new species arose. The Jurassic also marks the time when the cryptodirians, or hidden-necked turtles, made their appearance in the fossil record. The Jurassic not only hosted new turtle diversity, it is also known as the period when dinosaurs flourished and the first birds and mammals appeared.

Kayentachelys aprix is another species of turtle that lived during the Jurassic. It holds the distinction of being the earliest documented species of cryptodirian

This small tortoise, Stylemys nebrascensis, *was the first species of fossil tortoise to be described from the United States. Several have been found in Nebraska and South Dakota.*

*The forbears of the Zulia toad-headed turtle (*Batrachemys zuliae*) emerged during the Miocene epoch of the Cenozoic era, some 23 million years ago.*

turtle. However, a close contender for "earliest cryptodire" was unearthed in India in 2000. The fossil remains of *Indochelys spatulata* indicate that this newly discovered species is from the same era as *Kayentachelys*, but they are not members of the same family. It was determined that the new turtle from the Jurassic belonged to its own family: Indochelyidae. Several additional species of turtles emerged during the Jurassic, including the soft-shelled turtles of the family Trionychidae, which still exist today.

Chelonians of the Cretaceous

By the time the Cretaceous period arrived, turtle diversity had increased significantly. The oceans were active with a variety of fish and reptiles, including some spectacular examples of sea turtles.

The Cretaceous hosted a greater sea turtle diversity than is present today. Aside from more species of sea turtles, there were some that reached gigantic proportions. The now-extinct family Protostegidae was represented by at least nine genera, some of which were indeed giants. One noteworthy behemoth that patrolled the sea that once covered much of central North Amerca was *Protostega gigas*. These turtles reached lengths up to 11 feet (3.4 meters) in length. However, the title of largest prehistoric sea turtle belongs to the massive *Archelon ischyros*. This enormous chelonian grew to lengths exceeding 15 feet (4.6 meters). A living *Archelon* may have weighed as much as 4,000 pounds (2,200 kilograms)! As with other prehistoric chelonians, our knowledge of this turtle's lifestyle is limited to the information we can interpret from fossils. The curved beak of *Archelon* may have been useful in capturing squid and hard-shelled mollusks. Mollusk fossils are common in Cretaceous deposits and help us understand marine life during that period.

This Protostega gigas *fossil was found in north-central Texas. At 11 feet (3.4 meters) in length, it is the largest* Protostega *specimen ever collected. These prehistoric turtles used their hooked beaks to sift through the Cretaceous sea floor in search of invertebrates such as mollusks.*

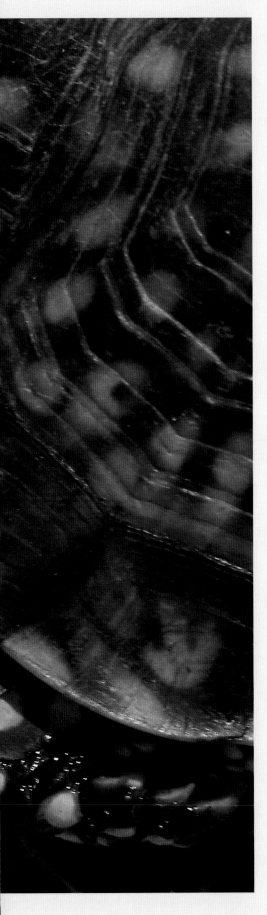

Part Two
The Diversity of Modern Chelonians

While the matamata (Chelus fimbriata) of South America appears peculiar on land, it blends perfectly in its underwater habitat, complete with aquatic vegetation and submerged leaf litter.

Left: *Of all turtle species, the three-toed box turtle (Terrapene carolina triunguis) demonstrates the highest amount of color variation.*

As if they were downward-pointed antennae, the chin barbels on this Hilaire's side-necked turtle (Phrynops hilarii) *serve as receptors to various environmental cues while the turtle is underwater.*

Some three hundred species of turtles inhabit the earth. Turtles can be found on every continent of the globe except Antarctica. These reptiles have established niches in diverse environments including prairies, deserts, forests, rivers, ponds, lagoons, lakes, swamps, and marshes in both tropical and temperate climates. Given such a successful repertoire, it is of little surprise that turtles have even established themselves as seaworthy occupants of the oceans.

Turtles belong to the class Reptilia and the order Testudines. This order consists of two easily distinguishable suborders: Cryptodiria and Pleurodira. The cryptodires are the hidden-necked turtles that are capable of retracting their necks within their shells via an S-shaped, or sigmoid, curvature of the vertebrae. Cryptodires account for eleven different families of turtles that possess eleven to twelve plastral scutes and eight to nine plastral bones. The Pleurodires are side-necked turtles represented by three families that fold their heads to the side instead of employing the more familiar method of neck retraction.

Eastern box turtle (*Terrapene carolina carolina*)

Northern Australian snake-necked turtle (*Macrochelodina rugosa*)

David C. Killpack

Turtles are grouped into two suborders based on the mechanics of their cervical vertebrae. The eastern box turtle is a hidden-necked turtle, or cryptodire. The northern Australian snake-necked turtle is a side-necked turtle, or pleurodire.

Chapter 4
Suborder Pleurodira
Side-Necked Turtles

Instead of retracting the head within the confines of the shell via vertical retraction of the vertebrae, a pleurodire turtle pulls its neck alongside the front of its shell by horizontally retracting the neck. This characteristic provides pleurodires with their common name, side-necked turtles. The shells of side-necked turtles are flattened and have thirteen plastral scutes and nine to eleven plastral bones. Another skeletal feature unique to side-necked turtles is a pelvis fused to the inside of the shell.

The future holds the prospect of discovering new side-necked species. Currently, three families, sixteen genera, and seventy-seven species represent the suborder Pleurodira. The most recent discovery was the Cann's snake-necked turtle (*Chelodina canni*), found only in Australia's Northern Territory. The scientific description of this species was published in 2002.

The natural habitat range of side-necked turtles includes the tropical climates of Africa, South America, Madagascar, and Australia. An exception to this rule occurs in Dade County, Florida, which is home to a localized population of East African black mud turtles (*Pelusios subniger*). This population comes from captive specimens that were released into the wild.

*A seemingly perpetual smile is present on the face of the matamata (*Chelus fimbriatus*) as it waits for fish to venture closer. The fleshy projections on its neck and the barbels hanging from its chin help the matamata detect the presence of prey.*
Matt Vaughn

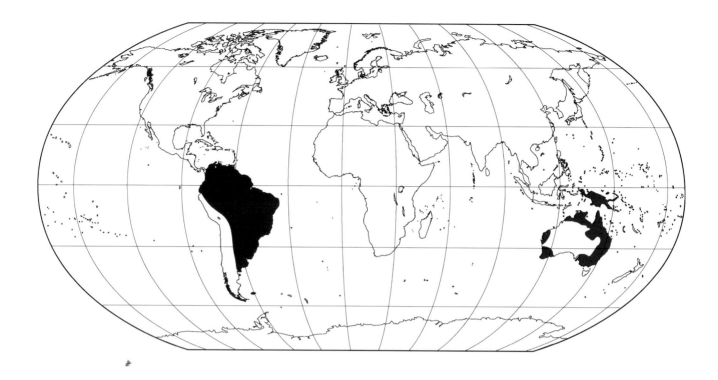

Another shared quality among side-necked turtles is an affinity for fresh water. Most side-necks have adapted nicely to an aquatic lifestyle. Some spend so much time in the water that they only venture onto land to lay eggs. Some even intentionally deposit their eggs underwater!

While pleurodires lead a life in close affiliation to the water, some are only semiaquatic. For example, the spiny-necked turtle (*Acanthochelys spixii*) and the twist-necked turtle (*Platemys platycephala*) of South America are semiaquatic. While other South American side-necked turtles patrol streams, rivers, and lakes, these semiaquatic species are poor swimmers and are content with ambling about creeks, swamps, and temporary pools of water within tropical rainforests.

Other side-necked turtles, such as helmeted turtles (*Pelomedusa subrufa*) and African hinged terrapins (*Pelusios* spp.), inhabit permanent or temporary bodies of fresh water. These turtles, like many others, are well adapted for passing the time during periods of drought. During the dry season, rising temperatures and a lack of rain cause many bodies of water in their habitat, including streams and rivers, to shrink dramatically or completely dry out. Turtles that live in

areas prone to drying bury themselves and essentially induce a state of suspended animation.

Family Chelidae
Austro-American Side-Necked Turtles

Comprising eleven genera and fifty-four species, the Austro-American side-necked turtles of the family Chelidae represent the greatest diversity among the pleurodires and have a geographic distribution that includes Australia, New Guinea, and tropical South America. Members of the family Chelidae range in size from the 5.5-inch (14-centimeters) western swamp turtle (*Pseudemydura umbrina*) to the 20-inch (50-centimeter) Mary River turtle (*Elusor macrurus*). These turtles are aquatic omnivores that are capable of producing clutches of one to twenty-five elongated or spherical brittle-shelled eggs. Of course, the number and size of the eggs depends on the size and species of the female. Most chelid turtles are well adapted for an aquatic lifestyle and inhabit bodies of fresh water such as rivers, lakes, ponds, swamps, creeks, and forest pools. Despite the fact that some chelid turtles are not efficient swimmers, all members of the family Chelidae live in or near aquatic environs.

Subfamily Chelidinae

Australia and New Guinea are inhabited by six genera of pleurodires belonging to the subfamily Chelidinae. Although Australia is the driest of the continents, it contains the greatest diversity of side-necked turtles. Given the lack of water in the Great Victorian Desert, it is of little surprise that turtles are virtually absent from Australia's central interior. With the exception of south-central Australia, turtle populations are present only in river drainages along the continent's coastline. Thirty-one species of chelid turtles occur in Australia; eight additional species occur in New Guinea.

During the Cenozoic era (37 million to 33.5 million years ago), the continent that would become Australia broke away and drifted northward from a portion of the former Gondwanaland supercontinent, now known as Antarctica, and has remained separated ever since. This isolation greatly influenced the evolutionary course of Australasia's flora and fauna. Among the distinctive evolutionary accomplishments in this part of the world is a unique group of turtles, the majority of which are side-necked. Aside from sea turtles, there is only one Australasian hidden-necked turtle, the Fly River turtle (*Carettochelys insculpta*).

Comprising two genera and thirteen species, the snake-necked turtles represent a major portion of Australasian turtle diversity. While they achieve their highest diversity in Australia, snake-necked turtles also occur in southern New Guinea. Snake-necked turtles are truly worthy of their common name. Some species, such as the narrow-breasted snake-necked turtle (*Chelodina oblonga*), have amazingly long necks that almost exceed the length of their shell, which reaches some 7 inches (17 centimeters). These turtles search for prey under rocks and into crevices by probing with their long and flexible necks. Other times, snake-

*The northern Australian snake-necked turtle (*Macrochelodina rugosa*) is a proficient swimmer and almost entirely aquatic. The female deposits her eggs into a nest that is completely underwater. Hatching occurs after the water dries, and the young leave their nest when the return of the rainy season softens the ground.*

necked turtles sit and wait underwater for an unsuspecting meal to venture close enough for an ambush, and then they strike in a rapid, snakelike manner.

Five genera compose the group known as the short-necked turtles. Short-necked turtles live in many of the same habitats where snake-necked turtles live. However, as their common name suggests, the necks of these side-necked turtles are short. Much like their snake-necked counterparts, the short-necked turtles display drab coloration, with one exception. The red-bellied short-necked turtle (*Emydura subglobosa*) of New Guinea and Australia has a beautiful pinkish-orange plastron and neck. This colorful turtle has become popular in the pet trade and among turtle hobbyists.

Five species represent the short-necked river turtles belonging to the genus *Emydura*. Adult females are typically larger in size than males and can reach lengths up to 13 inches (32 centimeters). Depending on the size of the female, *Emydura* are capable of producing seven to twenty round, brittle-shelled eggs per clutch.

In 1980, herpetologist John Legler and Australian turtle expert John Cann described an odd species of turtle inhabiting the Fitzroy River in Queensland. Overall, the Fitzroy River turtle (*Rheodytes leukops*) bears a typical chelonian appearance. However, the way it obtains most of its oxygen is anything but typical among turtles. All turtles have lungs, and some species possess cloacal bursae that assist with respiration. However, the Fitzroy River turtle receives as much as 70 percent of its oxygen intake directly from the water. The Fitzroy River turtle has an enlarged cloaca that connects to dual bursae, which are separated by a septum and lined with vascularized fimbriae. The fimbriae inside the bursae are rich in capillaries and absorb dissolved oxygen directly into the bloodstream while releasing carbon dioxide into the water.

Inguinal muscles pump water in and out of the cloaca. The water fills the bursae and muscular contractions pump it out. *Rheodytes* keeps the cloaca open while swimming and, according to Legler, the turtle's appearance while swimming is "reminiscent of an aircraft." *Rheodytes* relies heavily upon aquatic respiration. According to recent studies, *Rheodytes* can remain submerged underwater for ten hours and pumps 12 to 37 cubic inches (200 to 600 cc) of water in and out of its bursae at a rate of twenty to sixty times per minute.

The diet of *Rheodytes* consists primarily of aquatic arthropods including caddis fly and dragonfly larvae and crustaceans such as prawns. These invertebrates live beneath submerged rocks and are not a likely menu item for turtles that need to ascend to the surface for air. In addition, both the freshwater crocodile and the saltwater crocodile share the same river ecosystem as *Rheodytes*. The ability to remain submerged for long periods is likely beneficial for a turtle living among crocodiles.

Male Fitzroy River turtles are dimorphic and dichromatic. Males are distinguishable from females by their larger tails as well as the tint of orange on their heads, which brightens the otherwise drab body coloration.

Since the initial discovery of the Fitzroy River turtle, some populations have disappeared. The species requires fast-moving clean, clear water. Unfortunately, human activity has negatively altered portions of the river and caused much of the water to be turbid and unsuitable for *Rheodytes*. Due to its specific habitat preference and limited range, *Rheodytes leukops* is one of Australia's most endangered turtles.

Like the Fitzroy River turtle, the Mary River turtle (*Elusor macrurus*) of Queensland, Australia, is capable of absorbing dissolved oxygen directly from the water by using cloacal bursae. This turtle can attain a shell length up to 14 inches (35 centimeters). This species has not experienced the pressure of over-collection for the pet trade, but water pollution of the Mary River could detrimentally affect wild populations. Runoff from fertilizers, dredging of silt, and commercial mining for sand and gravel negatively affects underwater ecosystems in otherwise clean rivers.

Consisting of eight species, the genus *Elseya* represents the most diverse and widest ranging of the Australasian short-necked river turtles. Two species occur in Papua and Irian Jaya, while six occur only in Australia. Although these turtles are commonly referred to as "snapping turtles," they are not related to the North American snapping turtles that belong to the family Chelydridae.

The western swamp turtle (*Pseudemydura umbrina*), originally described in 1901, continues to defy extinction. This modestly sized brown turtle was rediscovered in 1954 after a young boy entered his interesting turtle in a pet show. It was soon realized that his pet was a rare species.

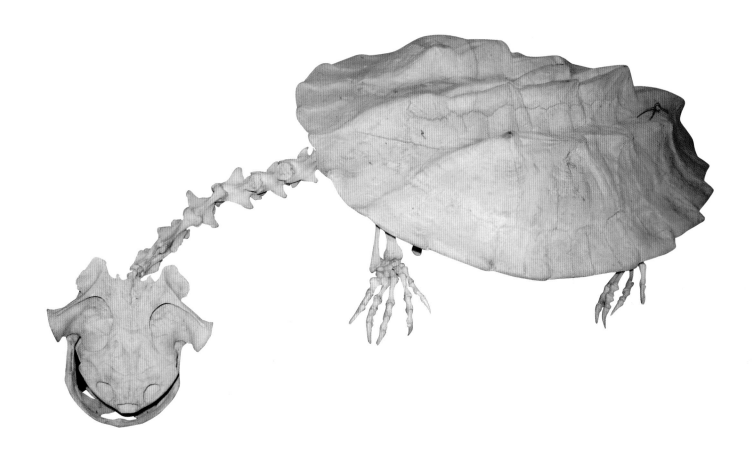

The skeleton of the matamata (Chelus fimbriatus) provides a clear view of the vertebrae used to support its long neck.

*Unlike the snake-necked turtles of Australia and Indonesia, the South American snake-necked turtle (*Hydromedusa tectifera*) of South America is not an adept swimmer. Instead, this species maintains a semiaquatic existence in swamps and flooded forests.*

The western swamp turtle is a carefully monitored species that is confined to one or two swamps near Perth in southwestern Australia. Australian and international conservation efforts aim to maintain viable populations of this endangered species in the wild.

Subfamilies Austrochelidinae and Hydromedusinae

While the cradle of chelid diversity rests within Australia and neighboring New Guinea, four genera and eight species of chelid turtles belonging to the subfamily Austrochelidinae inhabit South America. Two turtle species belonging to the subfamily Hydromedusinae also occur in South America. These turtles are widely distributed east of the

Andes Mountain Range from Colombia southward to Argentina.

Leading a low-key lifestyle in the slow-moving or stationary waters of South American creeks, rivers, swamps, and oxbow lakes is the matamata (*Chelus fimbriatus*). Of all the world's turtles, this one undoubtedly looks the weirdest. Matamatas display an incredible combination of physical characteristics that are designed to camouflage them within their natural environment. This bizarre-looking turtle can achieve shell lengths up to 18 inches (45 centimeters) and is equipped with a roughened carapace that bears protruding scutes. Complementing the odd shell, the sides of the limbs and neck of the matamata are festooned with an assortment of weird, fleshy ornamentation that help provide camouflage within

In traditional side-necked fashion, this Gibba turtle (Mesoclemmys gibba) *maintains an alert vigil even while its neck is retracted.*

its preferred environment of murky, leaf-filled waters. To complete the turtle's disguise, a broad triangular head is perched at the end of a long and thick neck. Even the protruding, snorkel-like nose of this turtle resembles the stem of a dead leaf. The head of the matamata is complete with more fleshy projections. The ornamentation on the limbs, neck, and head not only provide camouflage. Sensitive nerve endings on these projections help the turtle locate prey in murky waters.

Fish constitute a mainstay of the matamata's diet. When a complacent fish swims near the waiting head of a hungry matamata, the response is amazingly quick. With a movement that belies the species' otherwise sluggish nature, the neck slings forward and with a monumental gulp, it inflates to inhale the fish. No more than one second is required for this

event to happen. If we were to review a matamata feeding in slow motion, it would reveal a remarkable change in the turtle's appearance. After the head swings forward, the mouth expands to a size greater than the height of the head. Almost simultaneously, the neck swells from the presence of water combined with the inhalation of a fish. After it is all over, the matamata compresses the muscles in its neck and expels the excess water without losing its meal.

Four species of pleurodires belonging to the genus *Acanthochelys* occur throughout southeastern Brazil, Uruguay, Paraguay, eastern Bolivia, and northern Argentina. These side-necked turtles are poor swimmers and they reside in semiaquatic environments such as swamps and flooded forests. They have a drab overall coloration that provides camouflage in their swampy environment. Females produce

Side-Necked Turtles   61

*Geoffroy's side-necked turtle (*Phrynops geoffroanus*) inhabits slow-moving rivers, lakes, and other soft-bottomed bodies of water that have aquatic vegetation.*

between three to five spherical hard-shelled eggs per clutch.

Two snake-necked pleurodire species belonging to the genus *Hydromedusa* inhabit the swamps, ponds, marshes, and lakes of South America. Their flattened carapaces are brown, and the color of the limbs, neck, and head is charcoal gray. Webbing is present on each foot, which also bears four claws. The Brazilian snake-necked turtle (*Hydromedusa maximiliani*) can reach 8 inches (20 centimeters) in shell length and occurs in the Brazilian states of Espiritu Santo, Minas Gerais, Rio de Janeiro, and São Paulo. The South American snake-necked turtle (*H. tectifera*) has a geographic distribution that includes southeastern Brazil, Uruguay, Paraguay, and northeastern Argentina. It is the larger of the two species with adults reaching 11.8 inches (30 centimeters) in shell length.

A group of pleurodires widely referred to as toad-headed turtles resides in South America. Since the discovery of these turtles in the early 1800s, this group has undergone substantial taxonomic revision. Currently, six genera and fourteen species represent the toad-headed turtles. These aquatic turtles range in size from 8 to 17 inches (21 to 44 centimeters). They have round heads, tubular nostrils, and small barbels under the chin.

Depending upon the species, toad-headed turtles inhabit a variety of habitat types including slow-moving rivers, forest streams, water-filled ditches, quiet ponds, oxbow lakes, and flooded forests.

Six species compose the genus *Batrachemys*, otherwise known as the northern toad-headed turtles. Members of this genus have a geographic distribution stretching from southern Venezuela, western Brazil, northeastern Peru, and eastern Ecuador to southeastern Colombia and northern Bolivia. These moderately sized turtles reach lengths up to 13 inches (32 centimeters) and females lay as many as eight eggs per clutch.

Vanderhaege's toad-headed turtle (*Bufocephala vanderhaegei*) is a monotypic species, meaning that it is the sole member of its genus. This turtle reaches 11 inches (27 centimeters) in length and occupies rivers and swamps of Brazil, Paraguay, and Argentina.

The Gibba turtle (*Mesoclemmys gibba*) is another example of a monotypic toad-headed turtle. This species reaches 9 inches (23 centimeters) in length and inhabits the Orinoco and Amazon river basins of Colombia, eastern Ecuador, Peru, Venezuela, Guiana, northern Brazil, and Trinidad.

Gibba turtles are omnivorous, and females produce clutches of two to four elongated and brittle-shelled

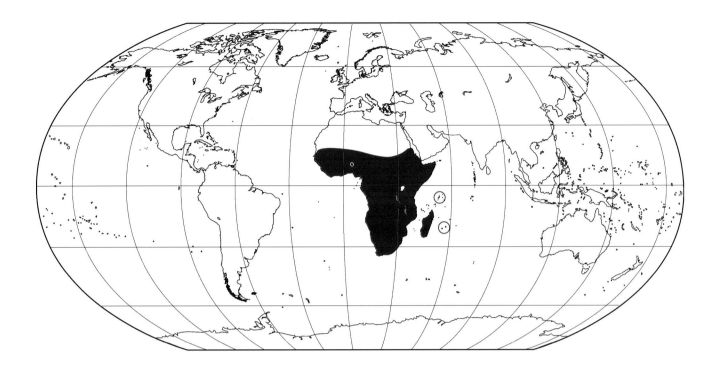

Range of the family Pelomedusidae

eggs that require up to two hundred days for incubation. When captured, this species bites and emits a foul-smelling musk.

Four species of bearded toad-headed turtles belong to the genus *Phrynops*. This group represents the widest-ranging genus of toad-headed turtles. They are found throughout almost the entire continent of South America east of the Andes to northeastern Argentina. Hilaire's side-necked turtle (*P. hilarii*) is the largest of the genus and can grow up to 17 inches (44 centimeters) in length.

The best known of the bearded toad-headed turtles is Geoffroy's side-necked turtle (*P. geoffroanus*). This species has a widespread distribution and the colorful pattern on its plastron has made it popular as a pet.

Hoge's side-necked turtle (*Ranacephala hogei*) is another monotypic species of toad-headed turtle. *R. hogei* possesses a domed and elongated carapace that reaches up to 14 inches (35 centimeters) in length. This species occupies low-elevation waterways of southeastern Brazil in the states of Espiritu Santo, Minas Gerais, and Rio de Janeiro.

The red side-necked turtle (*Rhinemys rufipes*) is also a monotypic species. This species inhabits black water and whitewater streams in southeastern Colombia and northeastern Brazil. Rainforests provide the origin of black water streams. As water slowly flows from the wet forest, acids and tannins are leached out of the decaying leaf litter and vegetation. This natural phenomenon results in transparent, yet tea-colored, water. Black water contains no water hardness and an acidic pH. *R. rufipes* rarely basks and spends a good deal of time on the bottom of waterways. Sometimes turtles of this species can be found hiding under moist leaf litter. The keeled carapace is oval-shaped with slight serrations on the posterior marginal scutes. Adults can attain lengths of 10 inches (26 centimeters), and females produce three to twelve spherical, brittle-shelled eggs per clutch.

Family Pelomedusidae

African Side-Necked Turtles

Two genera and nineteen species comprise the family Pelomedusidae, which has a geographic distribution that includes sub-Saharan Africa, Madagascar, and the Seychelles Islands north of Madagascar. A small

Hybridization sometimes occurs when various species are maintained together in captivity. This specimen is likely a cross between a West African mud turtle (Pelusios castaneus) *and an East African black mud turtle* (Pelusios subniger).

Groups of helmeted turtles (Pelomedusa subrufa) *sometimes attack prey simultaneously. This species is the only turtle species known to acquire food via a team effort.*

*The helmeted turtle (*Pelomedusa subrufa*), a monotypic species, is the only member of the family Pelomedusidae that does not possess a plastral hinge.*

population of East African black mud turtles (*Pelusios subniger*) that descended from pets that were released into the wild maintains a tenuous hold in southern Florida. Pelomedusid turtles are modest in size and have shell lengths ranging from 5 to 12 inches (12 to 30 centimeters). The shell is moderately domed, and a plastral hinge is present with all species of the genus *Pelusios*. Plastral hinges are not present on the helmeted turtle (*Pelomedusa subrufa*), a monotypic species.

African side-necked turtles inhabit stationary bodies of water such as marshes, ponds, and lakes. During the dry season when drought is imminent and water levels fall, they bury themselves in mud and aestivate until the onset of the rainy season. The female produces six to eighteen brittle- or leathery-shelled eggs, depending upon her size and species.

Pelomedusid turtles are primarily carnivorous but also opportunistically try other foods such as plant matter. As a testimony to their less-than-selective diets, these turtles even approach mammals such as rhinoceros and elephants that are taking a refreshing soak. Upon reaching the soaking behemoths, the turtles inspect their skin for blood-engorged ticks and other delectable ectoparasites. African hinged terrapins (*Pelusios* spp.) are also effective scavengers that heartily devour carrion.

Helmeted turtles (*Pelomedusa subrufa*) are the only turtles known to capture prey using a team effort. Whether this technique derives from any amount of premeditation, or simply from mutual hunger, is unknown. Nevertheless, the strategy is simple. The turtles wait near the shore for a suitably sized bird to approach. When the right bird arrives, the hungry turtles wait for it to lower its head for a drink. Once the animal is distracted, the turtles simultaneously rush the unsuspecting prey. The noise and commotion caused by the struggling bird invariably attracts the attention of more turtles, who rush to inspect the scene. A chain reaction results and more turtles pile onto the struggling creature.

Family Podocnemidae
South American River Turtles and the Madagascan Big-Headed Turtle

Turtles of the family Podocnemidae occur in the northern half of South America, east of the Andes, and in western Madagascar. Three genera and eight species represent this family. Podocnemids are aquatic turtles that have domed, streamlined shells. The turtles range in shell length from the modest 10-inch (25-centimeter) red-headed river turtle (*Podocnemis erythrocephala*) to the

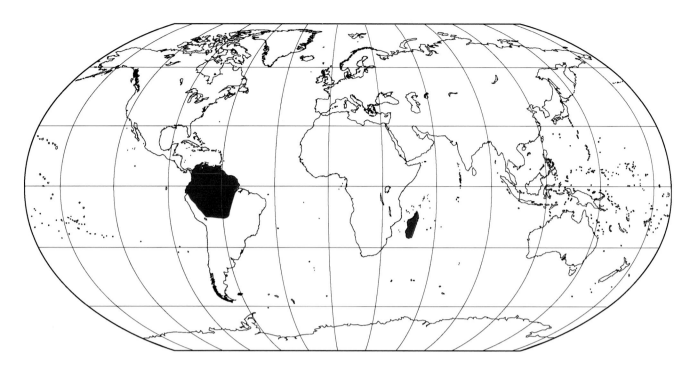

Range of the family Podocnemidae

32-inch (80-centimeter) South American river turtle (*Podocnemis expansa*). Podocnemid turtles are opportunistic feeders that consume a wide variety of food items including plants, fruits, slow-moving invertebrates, and carrion.

Every year in Brazil, South American river turtles that are also known as Arrau arrive by the hundreds at their traditional nesting locations on the Amazon and Orinoco riverbanks. Due to past harvesting of this species, some historic nesting sites are visited by a relatively small number of females. Arrau prefer to nest on large, sandy riverbanks. By using all four feet, the female swings scoop after scoop of sand out of the riverbank until she has excavated a nest chamber. Then she deposits eighty to one hundred leathery spherical eggs. Hatching usually takes place after fifty days of incubation.

Even though *P. expansa* nests at night, the species remains highly vulnerable to humans. For countless centuries, humans have relied upon this particular river turtle as a food source. Persistent and unregulated exploitation has caused a significant decline in its numbers. Documentation of the Arrau's decline dates as far back as 1863. During the early nineteenth century, the Arrau was exploited extensively for meat and eggs. Both adults and hatchlings were consumed, and oil was extracted from the eggs and sold for

cooking and fueling lamps. To comprehend the level of exploitation, consider that during one season an incredible five thousand jars of oil were collected from three nesting beaches. It is estimated that 33 million eggs were required to produce the five thousand jars of oil!

The Arrau consumes fallen fruits, seeds, and vegetation. Like other herbivorous turtles, the Arrau disperses seeds through its feces, which makes it an ecologically significant species. What environmental changes will occur, or have already occurred, now that this species has diminished? While it is difficult for us to imagine today, the Arrau of the nineteenth century were more abundant and even larger in size. It has also been reported that the Arrau of yesteryear produced more eggs. Instead of dozens or hundreds of these large turtles, imagine thousands arriving at the river beaches under the cover of darkness.

The yellow-spotted river turtle (*Podocnemis unifilis*) is another species that has been subject to human exploitation. This species has not experienced the same level of exploitation suffered by the Arrau or the systematic harvest of its eggs; however, yellow-spotted river turtles are relished for their meat. Reportedly, this species has the best-tasting flesh of the genus. The yellow-spotted river turtle is herbivorous and attains a carapace length of 27 inches (68 centimeters).

*The red-headed river turtle (*Podocnemis erythrocephala*) is primarily herbivorous, consuming ripe fruits that have fallen into the water.*

The Magdalena River turtle (*Podocnemis lewyana*) of Colombia is another example of a South American podocnemid that has been negatively affected by the overconsumption of its eggs and meat. This species lives in rivers, lagoons, swamps, and floodplains. It can reach a length of 18 inches (45 centimeters). Hopefully, recent investigations regarding the status of wild populations will provide more information about this diminishing species. The decline of the species is linked to its limited range within the Magdalena River basin of Colombia. Of the six species of South American podocnemids, this is the only one not found in the Amazon or Orinoco basins.

One of the smallest and most attractive of the podocnemids is the red-headed river turtle (*Podocnemis erythrocephala*). Attaining a length of 10 inches (25 centimeters) to 13 inches (32 centimeters), this olive brown turtle is adorned with a vivid crimson head that is offset by dark areas around the eyes, which are connected by a dark line extending across the back of the head. The vivid, red coloration becomes darker and more subtle among older specimens. This species is an inhabitant of black water habitats in the drainages of the Amazon and Orinoco rivers.

Another small member of this family is the six-tubercled Amazon River turtle (*Podocnemis sextuberculata*). As its common name suggests, this species occurs in the drainages of the Amazon River and sports six knob-like projections, or tubercles, on its shell. The tubercles occur in three pairs on the plastron. A single chin barbel is also characteristic of this turtle.

While most of the South American podocnemids are strong swimmers, the savanna side-necked turtle (*Podocnemis vogli*) prefers the grassy plains, called

*The six-tubercled Amazon River turtle (*Podocnemis sextuberculata*) sports a single chin barbel.*

llanos, of Venezuela and Colombia where it can be found in small streams, ponds, rivers, and swamps.

The big-headed Amazon River turtle (*Peltocephalus dumerilianus*) is an interesting chelonian that inhabits the Amazon basin of Peru, Colombia, and Venezuela and the Orinoco basin of Venezuela. This distinctive turtle can reach 27 inches (68 centimeters) in length and possesses a large, bony head. Half of its diet comprises fish, whereas the other South American podocnemids chiefly consume plants.

The Madagascan big-headed turtle (*Erymnochelys madagascariensis*) is the only member of the family Podocnemidae found in the Eastern Hemisphere. A fully grown Madagascan big-headed turtle can weigh up to 33 pounds (15 kilograms). The carapace is flat and reaches 18.5 inches (47 centimeters) in length. These turtles inhabit slow-moving rivers, lakes, and marshes in the northern to western lowlands of Madagascar.

The Madagascan big-headed turtle is among the twenty-five most endangered species of turtles. Scientists first noticed a threat to *E. madagascariensis* from high levels of fishing in 1982. Studies support the correlation between high levels of fishing and the depletion of Madagascan big-headed turtle populations. Malagasy law now protects the species from commercial trade. Unfortunately, despite legal protection, the species continues to suffer a high rate of incidental drowning in fishing nets.

*The savanna side-necked turtle (*Podocnemis vogli*) is a common inhabitant of ponds and swamps in Venezuela.*

Chapter 5
Suborder Cryptodira
Hidden-Necked Turtles

Cryptodires, or hidden-necked turtles, are defined by the ability to retract their necks within their shells via an S-shaped, or sigmoid, curvature of the vertebrae. Many of the hidden-necked turtles can retract their heads completely within their shell, while other species can retract their heads only partially. The snapping turtles (family Chelydridae), the big-headed turtles (family Platysternidae), the sea turtles (family Cheloniidae), some tortoises (family Testudinidae), and the soft-shelled turtles (family Trionychidae) cannot fully retract their heads inside their shells. Nonetheless, these turtles still possess a neck with the vertebrae positioned in a sigmoid arrangement. One exception is the leatherback sea turtle (family Dermocheylidae), which has a short and nonretracting neck. Cryptodires account for eleven different families of turtles, all of which have eleven to twelve plastral scutes and eight to nine plastral bones. The cryptodires are well suited for a wide variety of habitats; they are more diverse and widespread than the side-necked turtles.

*Ornate box turtle (*Terrapene ornata*).*
David C. Killpack

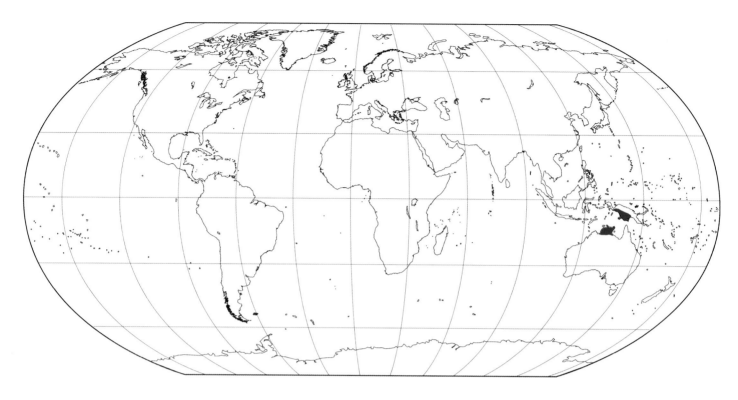

Family Carrettochelyidae
The Fly River Turtle

The Fly River turtle (*Carettochelys insculpta*), also known as the pig-nosed turtle, is the only known living member of the family Carrettochelyidae. Fossils dating back to the Eocene epoch (some 55 million to 34 million years ago) indicate that this family had a distribution that once included North America and Europe. These heavy-bodied turtles can attain a carapace length in excess of 24 inches (60 centimeters) and weigh up to 50 pounds (22.5 kilograms).

C. *insculpta* inhabits the meandering rivers and streams within the rainforests of New Guinea and northern Australia. The species was originally discovered in 1886 in a tributary flowing into the Fly River of Papua New Guinea. For several years, this incredible freshwater turtle was considered the rarest turtle in the world.

Instead of having a typical shell with tough carapacial scutes, the Fly River turtle possesses a leathery shell with a flexible rim. Juveniles display a keel and serrations on the margins of the carapace. While the shell is undoubtedly noteworthy, it is not exactly what makes this turtle unusual.

Even the tail of Carettochelys, *bearing twelve overlapping scales, is distinctive from that of other turtles.*

The soft underside of the Fly River turtle's plastron is often pinkish, providing a stark contrast to the dark carapace.

Matt Vaughn

With its leathery carapace, odd snout, and front flippers, the Fly River turtle (Carettochelys insculpta) *is indeed a curious species of freshwater turtle.*

The forelimbs resemble flippers and propel the turtle through the water. The form of the forelimbs is similar to that of the sea turtles, and each bears two claws. The hind feet are paddle-shaped and only have one claw. The dorsal surface of the tail is covered with a series of twelve overlapping scales. The unusual nose provides this species with its other common name, pig-nosed turtle. The fleshy snout is trunk-like and has nostrils located at the very tip.

The Fly River turtle's carapace and dorsal surfaces of the head, neck, limbs, and tail vary from slate gray to olive in color. The plastron and ventral surfaces are creamy beige to pinkish white in some specimens, and almost completely pink in others. This coloration is also present on a spot on the sides of the head, behind each eye, and on the fleshy areas between limbs.

C. insculpta resides in bodies of clear water as well as turbid waters. In turbid waters, olfactory functions likely help locate food items and potential mates. *Carettochelys* prefers a small river system with plentiful vegetation and a sandy bottom covered by a fine layer of silt, as well as lagoons and ponds. When approached by divers, Fly River turtles often remain motionless near overhanging banks or beneath fallen tree trunks. However, they can rapidly escape and are reportedly able to swim four times faster than a human.

Most of the Fly River turtle's distribution occurs in New Guinea. Although known as a freshwater inhabitant, *Carettochelys* shows a fair tolerance for brackish water. This capacity has given some scientists the notion that the species may have migrated from southern New Guinea to northern Australia. In 1905, a specimen was found swimming in salt water near the mouth of the Fly River. Aboriginal rock paintings of *Carettochelys* are present at the Khakadu National Park in the Northern Territory, Australia. Although these seven-thousand-year-old rock paintings are well known, the depictions of *C. insculpta* went unnoticed by herpetologists until 1970.

In the wild, this opportunistic feeder consumes a variety of aquatic vegetation such as ribbon weed, algae, and fallen fruits. Snails, prawns, insects, carrion, and other prey items also constitute a portion of the diet.

Unlike other freshwater turtles, *Carettochelys* swims in a manner similar to that of sea turtles. Both forelimbs simultaneously stroke upward and downward as the turtle "flies" through the water.

The sexes are easy to distinguish because males have a larger and longer tail, with the cloacal opening extending beyond the rim of the carapace. Nesting takes place from September to November. The female typically selects a sandy stretch of riverbank into which she deposits as many as thirty spherical, brittle-shelled eggs per clutch. The smooth-shelled eggs are buried in a shallow nest and measure about 1.6 inches (40 millimeters) in diameter.

Hatchlings usually have a carapace length of 2.2 inches (57 millimeters) and emerge from their eggs at the onset of the summer rainy season. Laboratory tests have demonstrated that the young remain fully formed, yet dormant, in their eggs until monsoonal conditions arrive. It is possible that water levels inundating the nest, after the development of the young, trigger their emergence.

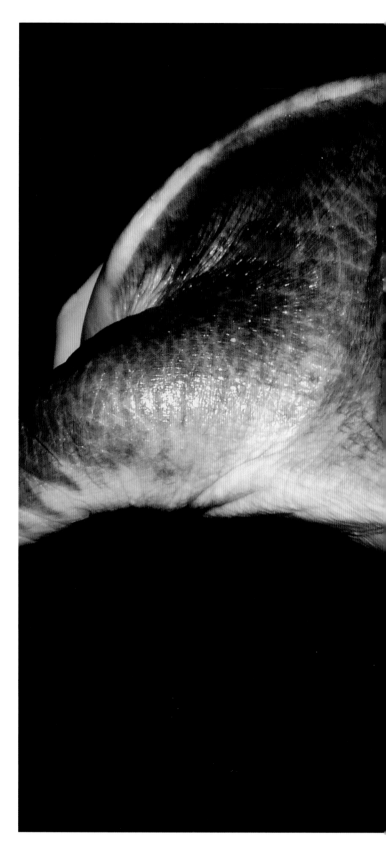

The tubular snout of Carettochelys insculpta *leaves little to the imagination as to how this turtle received the common name pig-nosed turtle.*

Matt Vaughn

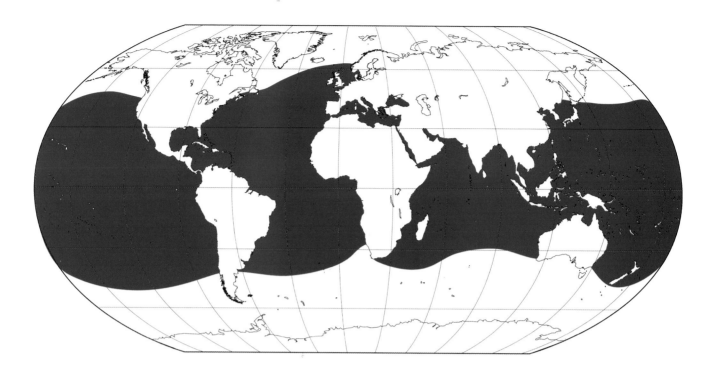

Range of the family Cheloniidae

Family Cheloniidae

Sea Turtles

Five genera and six species represent the living members of the family Cheloniidae. These marine turtles occur throughout most of the world, most commonly in warm tropical waters near a continental shelf or reefs. However, they do occasionally enter temperate regions of the oceans and seas.

These large turtles have a carapace covered in keratinized scutes and, depending upon the species in question, range in size from 30 inches (100 centimeters) to 39 inches (124 centimeters) and weigh as much as 95 pounds (43 kilograms) to 400 pounds (200 kilograms).

Sea turtles are specialized for their saltwater habitat and distinguishable from other turtles by a number of characteristics. One obvious feature is the shape of the forelimbs, which are modified into flippers. This feature is unique to sea turtles, with the exception of the freshwater Fly River turtle.

Salt excretion glands near the corner of the eye help sea turtles eliminate excessive amounts of salt that are ingested during feeding. These glands allow the sea turtle to maintain a healthy physiology in a saltwater environment.

Males rarely venture onto the beach and spend most of their lives in the water. Females are the only ones to come ashore with any regularity. Depending on the individual specimen, these visits to land may take place three to five times per year.

Like their ancestors before them, female sea turtles of today continue the age-old cycle of returning to their traditional nesting grounds under the cover of darkness to excavate their nests and deposit eggs.

During the mating season, the males congregate at their breeding grounds and wait for the females to arrive. Upon the arrival of the females, the males begin competing with one another for the opportunity to mate. When a male approaches a female, he climbs onto her carapace and holds on with his flippers and claws. He then wraps his tail around the female's tail and releases his sperm directly into her cloaca. Mating takes place in the water and the event can last for hours. A female that is not interested in mating retreats from the males, uses her hind flippers to cover the cloaca, or swims to the bottom and presses her plastron against the ocean floor. When a male succeeds in copulating with a female, other

David C. Killpack

Sea turtles frequent coral reef "cleaning stations," where saltwater species engage in mutualistic behavior. Here, surgeonfish, cleaner wrasse, shrimp, and a remora remove ectoparasites and dead skin from a green sea turtle (Chelonia mydas mydas).

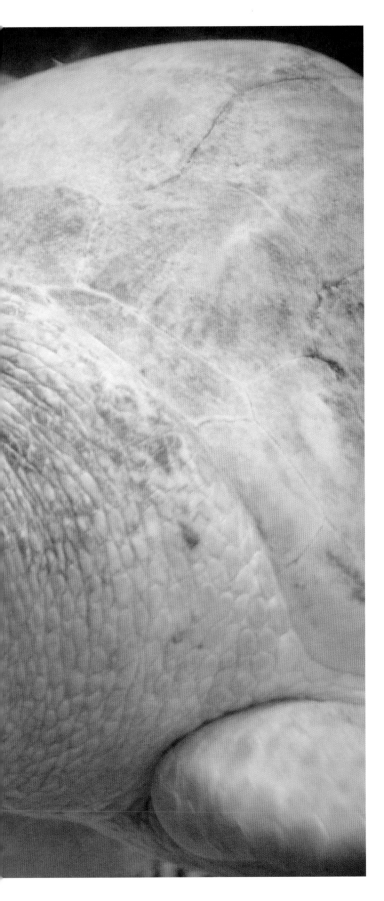

*The common name of the green sea turtle (*Chelonia mydas mydas*) has nothing to do with its external coloration. Instead, it is the green body fat that earns the turtle its name.*

males sometimes attack the copulating male by ramming and biting him. If these actions discourage the male during mating, another suitor will replace him.

Female sea turtles head to the beaches when it is time to lay their eggs. Using her hind feet, the turtle excavates a flask-shaped tunnel where she deposits 50 to 160 leathery, spherical eggs per clutch. After depositing her eggs, she leaves the nest and is unlikely to ever see any of her offspring.

As with most turtles, the sex of a developing sea turtle embryo is determined by temperature. Although the exact temperatures required to create a male or female vary slightly between species, a general rule of thumb applies. Typically, eggs incubated at a temperature not exceeding 84 degrees Fahrenheit (29 degrees Celsius) result in mostly males, while those incubated at higher temperatures—between 85 and 89 degrees Fahrenheit (29.6 to 32 degrees Celsius)—result in most or all of the eggs hatching as females.

One of the greatest phenomena surrounding the sea turtle's reproductive cycle is that females return to the same nesting location every time. Amazingly, these nesting locations are believed to be the very beaches where the females first crawled out of the sand as hatchlings and entered the water. Exactly how the turtles accomplish this feat, after swimming hundreds or even thousands of miles from their birthplace, remains a mystery.

The loggerhead sea turtle (*Caretta caretta*) is the largest member of the family Cheloniidae and has a geographic distribution that includes most of the world's oceans except for the eastern and central Pacific. Fully grown loggerheads can attain a shell length up to 49 inches (124 centimeters) and weigh as much as 440 pounds (200 kilograms).

The carapace is yellowish brown and the plastron is creamy yellow. These turtles earn their common name from their massive heads, which are adapted for crushing hard-shelled prey items such as horseshoe crabs and mollusks. The nesting grounds for loggerhead sea turtles are located on the coastlines of the southeastern United States, Australia, the eastern Mediterranean, and Brazil.

The green sea turtle (*Chelonia mydas mydas*) inhabits most of the world's tropical oceans and seas, and the black sea turtle (*Chelonia mydas agassizi*) occurs near the Pacific shorelines. Previously, the black and the green sea turtles were thought to represent separate species. However, physical and molecular data have proved this claim unsubstantiated. Both turtles are now categorized as subspecies of *Chelonia mydas*. While the black sea turtle earned its common name from its shell color, the green sea turtle received its name from the greenish color of its body fat.

The black and the green sea turtles have a small, round head and a smooth carapace. These turtles can grow up to 48 inches (122 centimeters) in shell length and weigh as much as 450 pounds (204 kilograms). Aside from occasional invertebrates, their diet is mostly herbivorous. Serrated cusps greatly assist these turtles in making a feast of sea grass and algae.

C. mydas returns to nesting locations on beaches in Florida, the Caribbean, islands of the eastern Pacific, Australia, the Persian Gulf, and Malaysia.

With a maximum shell length of 39 inches (99 centimeters) and a mass up to 198 pounds (90 kilograms), the hawksbill sea turtle (*Eretmochelys imbricata*) ranges throughout most of the world's tropical seas. This species is the most ornamental of the sea turtles. The carapace bears a rich, amber hue offset by a series of dark brown to blackish lines that radiate on each scute. The plastron is whitish yellow. The carapacial scutes overlap one another, and the marginal scutes on the

posterior portion of the body are notably serrated. Two claws are present on each of the front flippers. The extended and curved beak of this species is what provides the hawksbill sea turtle with its common name.

Hawksbill sea turtles have nesting locations on beaches in the Caribbean, Yucatán Bahia, Brazil, the Persian Gulf, the Seychelles Islands, Malaysia, Indonesia, and Australia.

Another distinctive species of sea turtle inhabits the warm oceans near the northern coast of Australia as well as the Gulf of Papua. The flatback sea turtle (*Natator depressus*) has a grayish to olive brown flattened carapace and a creamy, tan plastron. Flatbacks can grow to 39 inches (99 centimeters) in shell length and weigh as much as 198 pounds (90 kilograms). These turtles avoid coral reefs and primarily consume jellyfish, sea pens, and other soft-bodied invertebrates.

Because of its confined distribution and use of remote nest sites that are free of human activity, the flatback is the least studied of the sea turtles. All of the known nesting locations for flatback sea turtles are within Australia and include Queensland, Crab Island, and the Northern Territory.

With a maximum carapace length of 30 inches (76 centimeters), the smallest of the sea turtles are the ridleys (*Lepidochelys* spp.). Two species belong to the genus *Lepidochelys*. Kemp's ridley sea turtle (*L. kempii*) has an olive green carapace and a creamy yellow plastron. This species occurs in the northern Atlantic Ocean to the Caribbean Sea; it is the rarest and most endangered of the sea turtles.

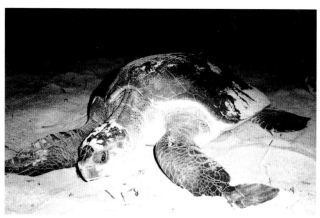

Shreyas Krishnan

*While all species of sea turtles have suffered notable population declines, the olive ridley (*Lepidochelys olivacea*) remains the most abundant of the world's sea turtles.*

Human hunger often supersedes conservation laws. These hunters on the Andaman Islands of India carry out a millennia-old ritual of Homo sapiens *consuming turtles. The feast is a large female green sea turtle (*Chelonia mydas mydas*).*

Shreyas Krishnan

Female Kemp's ridleys nest primarily at Ranch Nuevo, Tamaulipas, Mexico. Throughout much of the twentieth century, a turtle slaughterhouse was present at this location. The meat and hides of these turtles were sold here, which contributed greatly to the decline of the species. An estimated 42,000 nesting females were recorded at this location in 1947; by 1990, the number was just over 500. It was not until 1990 that the Mexican government closed down the slaughterhouse. By then, the facility was responsible for extirpating more endangered turtles than any single operation in the world.

While the Kemp's ridley is the rarest of the sea turtles, fortunately the same cannot be said for the olive ridley sea turtle (*Lepidochelys olivacea*). This turtle is similar in appearance to Kemp's ridley and has a geographic distribution that includes the Pacific and Indian oceans and the Atlantic west of Africa and east of South America. In fact, the olive ridley is the most common of all sea turtles with nesting locations on beaches in India, Mexico, and Costa Rica.

The Perils of Being a Sea Turtle

Sea turtles are in imminent danger of extinction, and it is entirely due to the actions of humans. Our race has single-handedly done more to eradicate various animal and plant species than any other in recorded history.

While international conservation laws have been passed with the intention of preserving sea turtles, these laws are only effective if they are obeyed and enforced. For the most part, they are not. To this day, the flesh and eggs of sea turtles are taken for human consumption; skins and shells are sold as souvenirs in the forms of artwork; jewelry is fashioned from shells; and entire stuffed specimens are sold for profit. Some of these practices continue due to legal loopholes, while other infractions are direct violations. The lack of legal enforcement stems from a range of factors. These include, but are not limited to, officials who are sympathetic to the actual survival needs of people; officials who are unaware of the scope of the problems concerning sea turtles; corrupt officials; and, in some locations, legal problems superseding the importance of protecting turtles.

Aside from the direct impact of the harvest and consumption of adults and eggs, sea turtles are challenged further by habitat loss and pollution. One victim of pollution is the leatherback sea turtle. These giant turtles have been found dead from starvation. The culprit is often a belly full of plastic bags, which the turtle mistook for jellyfish and subsequently consumed. Since they are unable to digest the plastic, the leatherback accumulates the bags until they fill the stomach. Ultimately, the turtle dies from starvation with a full stomach of plastic bags. Leatherbacks suffer greatly from this form of pollution, and other sea turtle species are known to suffer from the same type of problem.

While the ingestion of plastic bags and other foreign objects are some examples of visible pollutants, certain invisible vectors are equally opportunistic in their prejudice against sea turtles. The primary culprit in this category is a herpes-like virus responsible for the condition known as fibropapillomatosis (FP). FP is

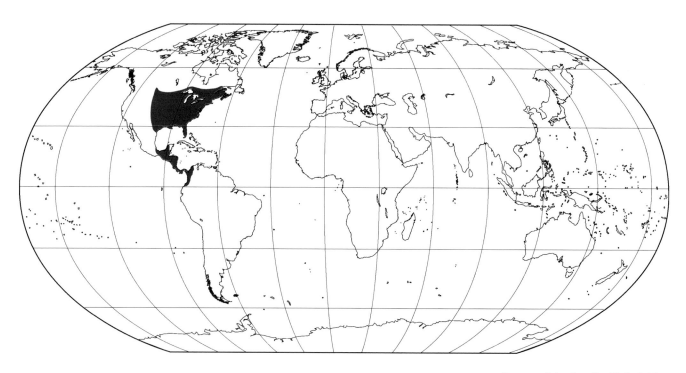

characterized by an infestation of benign tumors on the dermal and epidermal layers of the skin.

The first documented incident of a sea turtle being infected with FP was documented in 1938. Since then, researchers have discovered many populations of the green sea turtle (*Chelonia mydas mydas*) infected with FP. While green sea turtles seem to constitute the largest percentage of victims, other species such as the hawksbill (*Eretmochelys imbricata*), the flatback (*Natator depressus*), and the Kemp's and olive ridley (*Lepidochelys* spp.) have been found infected with FP.

The first signs of an infection from these tumors are often found in the eyes. During the initial stages of development, the tumors emerge from out of the corner of the eyes. The tumors can occur virtually anywhere on the body of the turtle.

While numerous sea turtles afflicted with this condition have received therapeutic attention for external tumors, little can be done for those turtles that have severe internal tumor growth. When the tumors grow inside, they risk killing the turtle by interfering with the function of the organ system. Necropsies of recently deceased specimens have revealed tumors inside the heart, stomach, and other organs. In one instance, a dead turtle was found with tumors filling its esophagus and growing within the oral cavity of its mouth. One can only imagine the amount of suffering that the turtle endured before dying of starvation or asphyxiation.

Researchers have recently documented an interesting trend suggesting that sea turtles infected with FP at an older age and of larger size tend to recover more quickly than younger, smaller individuals.

Family Chelydridae

Snapping Turtles

With a ridged carapace, juxtaposed scutes, a greatly reduced cross-shaped plastron, well developed limbs, webbed feet with claws, a long tail covered in plate-like scales topped off with a row of dorsally oriented serrated scales, and a large head bearing a strongly cusped beak, Chelydrid turtles are undeniably easy to recognize. The family Chelydridae is represented by two species, the common snapping turtle (*Chelydra serpentina*) and the alligator snapping turtle (*Macrochelys temminckii*). On both species, the carapace has three noticeable ridges running its length. These ridges are comprised of the ridges found on each of the scutes on the carapace. The ridges are worn smooth over time and tend to be less prominent among older specimens. The scutes on the posterior portions of the carapace are serrated, a characteristic that also becomes reduced with advancing age.

A thick and powerful neck supports the large head. The length of the neck varies between the two

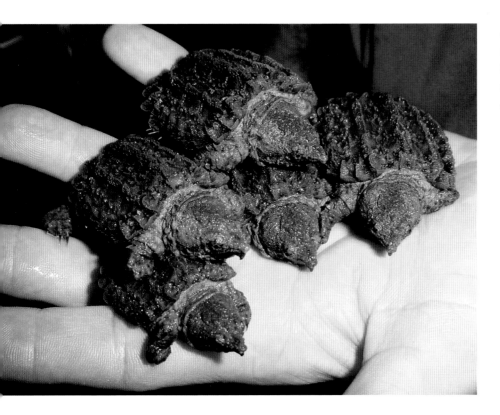

Amazingly, these hatchling alligator snapping turtles (Macrochelys temminckii) can grow into the largest species of freshwater turtle in North America.

Snapping turtles are superb hunters and scavengers. This individual was found in Parker County, Texas, with its entire body concealed and ready to ambush unsuspecting prey.

species. Common snapping turtles have a longer neck than alligator snapping turtles. Alligator snapping turtles can extend their necks to a limited extent, but not to the degree that a common snapping turtle can. Both species use the neck to propel the heavy head and sharp cusp with lightning speed.

The alligator snapping turtle is the largest of the snapping turtles as well as one of the largest species of freshwater turtle in the world. Adult males can attain carapace lengths up to 31 inches (80 centimeters) and weigh as much as 250 pounds (113 kilograms). The common snapping turtle is more modest in size, with adults attaining a maximum length of 19 inches (49 centimeters) and weighing as much as 86 pounds (39 kilograms). These big turtles are brownish gray in color and well adapted for a life patrolling the bottoms of creeks, lakes, ponds, rivers, and swamps. Common snapping turtles sometimes appear in brackish water.

The common snapping turtle has a geographic distribution that extends from southern Canada into the United States, east of the Rocky Mountains, and southward into Mexico, Central America, and Ecuador. Of the two species, alligator snapping turtles occupy a smaller range and are restricted to river systems in the southeastern United States.

Although primarily aquatic, snapping turtles occasionally leave the water to bask or venture about on land. This activity most commonly occurs after heavy rains, during drought when individuals are searching for water, or when females are looking for nesting sites. Ponds, slow-moving creeks and rivers, lakes, and brackish marshes are suitable habitats for snapping turtles. A body of water with a soft, muddy bottom is preferred. In such environs, one can sometimes encounter snapping turtles covered in mud with only the eyes and nostrils exposed. In this position, the snapping turtle is well poised to ambush unsuspecting prey. Not only does its long neck allow the turtle to ambush prey, it also allows a concealed snapper to raise its nostrils to the surface without disturbing its hiding place.

*The common snapping turtle (*Chelydra serpentina*) uses its sensitive sense of smell to help locate prey underwater. Snapping turtles have even helped crime investigators locate drowning victims.*

Almost all bites from alligator snapping turtles occur after they have been captured, carelessly handled, or otherwise molested.

Alligator snapping turtles have an interesting method for securing fish. These turtles are capable of remaining submerged for well over an hour. When an alligator snapping turtle finds the right location, it sits motionless with its mouth agape. The coloration of the inside of the mouth matches that of the turtle and often the immediate surroundings, while a contrasting pink tongue offsets the muddy, charcoal-colored mouth. Unlike the broad and fleshy tongue of the common snapping turtle, the tongue of the alligator snapping turtle is small and forked. While the motionless turtle gapes, the tongue flickers, twists, and flops with muscular contractions not unlike those of a drowning earthworm. Once a fish ventures too close to the flickering morsel, the trap is sprung and the enormous jaws slam shut.

Both species of snapping turtle are opportunistic feeders known to consume a wide variety of food items including duckweed, water hyacinth, algae, water lettuce, mollusks, crustaceans, insects, carrion, fish, amphibians, reptiles, birds, and small mammals. Snapping turtles have even been used to locate drowning victims in lakes. In such instances, long wires were attached to the shells of snapping turtles. Once the scavenging chelonians located the remains of the deceased, the investigators could recover the bodies.

In general, snapping turtles are calm underwater and try to flee in the presence of a person. However, these powerful turtles can effectively defend themselves when confronted in the water. They are capable of aggressively defending themselves on land as well. If molested, a snapping turtle opens its mouth and raises its hind legs. This elevated position allows it to lunge toward an aggressor.

Family Dermatemydidae

The Central American River Turtle

The Central American river turtle (*Dermatemys mawii*) is the only living member of the family Dermatemydidae. Remains dating back to the Cretaceous period and Miocene epoch from Europe, North America, and East Asia indicate that this family of turtles was once more widely represented than it is today.

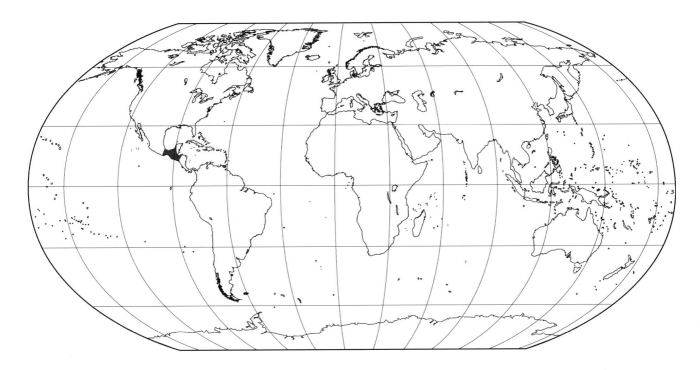

Range of the family Dermatemydidae

This large, freshwater turtle may be capable of reaching a carapace length of 25.5 inches (65 centimeters) and weigh in excess of 48 pounds (22 kilograms). Central American river turtles have a geographic distribution that includes Vera Cruz and northern Oaxaca, Mexico, to the Yucatan Peninsula, Belize, and eastern Guatemala.

Juveniles possess a keel in the center of the carapace. As the turtle ages, the keel disappears and the shell assumes a smoother appearance. The smooth appearance of the carapace is also due to the leathery layer of skin covering the shell. The plastron is large, unhinged, and connected to the carapace by a wide bridge. The toes are strongly webbed and a series of enlarged scale fringes are present on the outer margins of each foot.

The carapace of the Central American river turtle is brown to olive, and the plastron is creamy yellow. Occasionally, dark suffusions are present on the posterior margins of the plastron. Males have a head that is yellowish to reddish brown. The colors contrast from the brown to olive coloration typically found on the sides and bottom of the head and neck. In females, the head and neck are gray to olive, with the jaws and throat bearing a creamy yellow coloration. Juveniles are colored slightly different from the adults. The head of a young specimen is light brown to olive, with a yellowish orbital stripe. The dorsal surface of juveniles is brownish to olive, and the ventral surface is yellowish.

Through out its range, *D. mawii* inhabit permanent bodies of water such as creeks, rivers, and freshwater lagoons. This species is primarily vegetarian and active mainly at night. Although these turtles may engage in limited terrestrial movements, they are better suited for a life in the water and have a difficult time moving out of the water. During the day, sleeping specimens are sometimes found floating at the water's surface. Due to the mainly aquatic nature of this turtle's lifestyle, nasopharyngeal respiration likely serves as an important function. Captive specimens have been observed gulping water into their mouths while expelling water through their nostrils. This is a mode of respiration similar to buccopharyngeal respiration. However, instead of having vascular tissue in the mouth and neck designed to absorb oxygen, *Dermatemys* has vascular tissue in part of the pharynx above the level of the soft palate.

Since terrestrial movement is difficult for this species, females lay their eggs close to the shore. It is

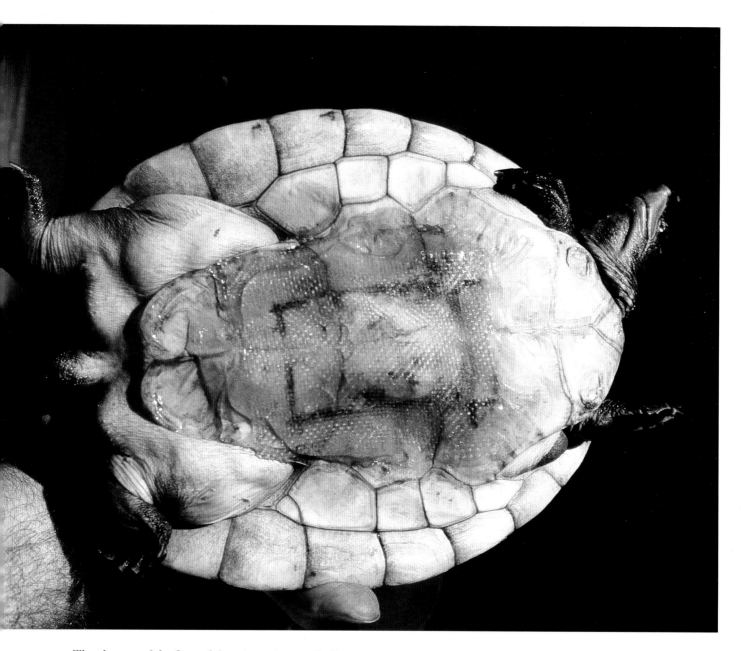

The plastron of the Central American river turtle (Dermatemys mawii) is soft and vulnerable to injury. This specimen had worn a hole in its plastron after walking on a concrete floor. Veterinarians used a fiberglass patch to repair the damage.

Right: *The Central American river turtle (Dermatemys mawii) is threatened with extinction due to overhunting for food.*

David C. Killpack

not uncommon for the eggs to become submerged when water levels rise. Fortunately, eggs of *D. mawii* can remain viable while underwater for up to twenty-seven days.

The Central American river turtle faces the threat of extinction throughout much of its range. Adults are often captured for food. Since the turtles spend most of their days floating while asleep, they make conspicuous targets for attentive fishermen.

Sadly, many of the laws and regulations that are respected by most in the scientific community are not a priority over the rumbling of hungry stomachs. To this day, one can still purchase meat from *Dermatemys* without penalty! A friend of mine once received all of the permits necessary from the government of Guatemala to export a few live specimens to the United States. These turtles were purchased from restaurants where they were awaiting a certain fate. Ironically, the troubles did not manifest until the turtles were brought into the United States. An USFWS agent refused clearance of the specimens, despite their accompanying permission for export by the Guatemalan government! His reasoning was that the

turtle was an endangered species. Shortly thereafter, the USFWS turned over their "evidence" to a local zoo. Interestingly enough, it was the same zoo that the scientist had intended as a home for the delivered turtles.

Family Dermochelyidae

The Leatherback Sea Turtle

The leatherback sea turtle (*Dermochelys coriacea*) is the largest living and most widespread species of turtle. Adults can grow to just over 6 feet (2 meters) in total body length and weigh as much as 2,016 pounds (913 kilograms)! The only living reptile that can surpass the size of these marine behemoths is the saltwater crocodile, which can grow to 23 feet (7 meters) in length and weigh more than 3,000 pounds (1,400 kilograms).

This unique species is the most specialized of all the living turtles in the world. In fact, it was once classified in a group of reptiles separate from all other turtles. The most distinguishable characteristics

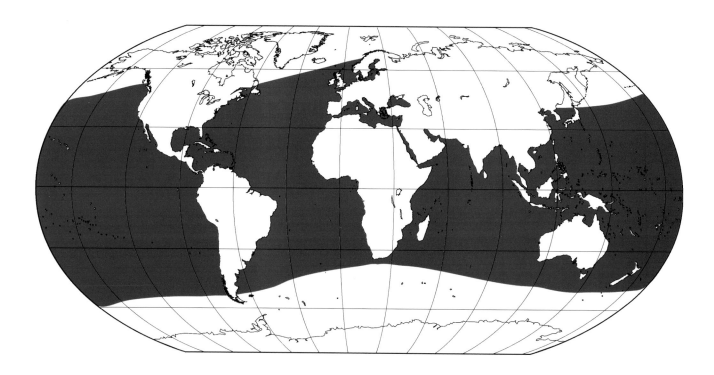

of *D. coriacea* are a carapace that lacks a hardened layer of horny scutes and a completely scale-free body. The bony elements of a leatherback's shell have been reduced to little more than a mosaic of small, irregularly shaped bones called ossicles. The resulting feel of their shell is that of thick, rubbery leather.

The coloration of the carapace may be slate gray, black, bluish black, or brown, with scattered white to yellowish specks. The head may be slate gray to black with speckling present. The chin and ventral portion of the neck are noticeably lighter in color and have a higher concentration of speckling. The limbs are grayish black with the heaviest amount of spotting on the anterior portions of the flippers.

The carapace is elongated and lyre-shaped; it tapers to a point just above the tail. The highest and widest point of the carapace is just above the shoulders. Five longitudinally oriented ridges formed of tightly fitted osteoderms run the length of the carapace, while a prominent medial keel extends the entire length of the shell. Shallow troughs are present between the dorsal ridges.

Leatherback hatchlings bear scales on the limbs and head. These scales are lost after the young turtles shed their skin at twenty-six and forty-six days of age. The limbs are devoid of any claws such as those found on the flippers of other sea turtles.

The ventral surface of the leatherback sea turtle is also relatively soft. In Suriname, South America, this characteristic has played a role in the occasional death of females. While venturing out of the Atlantic Ocean and onto beaches at night, they have accidentally impaled themselves on driftwood.

The head of the leatherback is large, and the neck is short and wide. This sturdy design affords very little flexibility but enhances the body's aerodynamics in the water.

The leatherback's digestive system is specialized to feed on the vast number of jellyfish that drift afloat in the oceans. The turtle's beak is tricuspid, and the inside of the mouth is lined with spiny, horny projections directed toward the rear of the mouth. These projections continue from the inside of the mouth into the looped esophagus, which can measure over 7 feet (2 meters) in length and has a descending and ascending portion. The internal organs, such as the esophagus and stomach, appear to be quite flexible considering that leatherbacks ingest vast amounts of seawater while consuming jellyfish, and then eject the former. The projections lining the esophagus and mouth help prevent the loss of the turtle's slippery feast when the water is expelled. Given the meager constitution of most jellyfish, it is mind-boggling to imagine the sheer volume of the invertebrates these

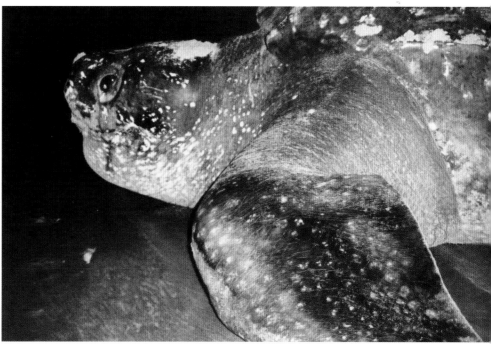

*Although categorized as a hidden-necked turtle, the leatherback sea turtle (*Dermochelys coriacea*) actually possesses a short, thick, nonretractable neck.*

enormous turtles must consume to satisfy their nutritional requirements.

Beneath the leathery flesh and ossicles of the carapace is a large amount of cartilage that is rich in blood vessels. Unlike other turtle species, the ribs of *Dermochelys* are not fused to the inside of the carapace. Instead, they are buried within a layer of cartilage, fat, and ossicles.

The family Dermochelyidae is known from fossil deposits from the Eocene epoch. Recently, scientists have begun to understand more regarding the past diversity of leatherback turtles; however, one major obstacle challenges these paleotological pursuits. The habitat and body of a prehistoric creature greatly affects how and where its remains settled. *Dermochelys* has always dwelled in the open oceans, and its carapace has always been comprised of a mosaic of bony plates. While the remains of some ancient leatherbacks fossilized, it is likely that many more simply decomposed amid the elements and the scavengers of the ocean.

What *is* known about these ancient turtles is that there were at least four genera and nine species belonging to the family Dermochelyidae. Just as more leatherback fossils are likely to be discovered eventually, a better insight into the past of this now monotypic family will be gained.

While *Dermochelys* is a type of sea turtle, it can be more accurately described as a marine reptile. Unlike the other sea turtles, the leatherback does not inhabit the continental shelf or reefs. Instead, it is truly a restless wanderer of the open seas.

The leatherback sea turtle has a worldwide distribution and occurs in all temperate and tropical oceans. These turtles routinely travel great distances and can move at a rate of 112 miles (70 kilometers) per day. One specimen that was tagged during a study of nesting females in Suriname was found four months later and 2,700 miles (4,345 kilometers) away in the cold waters off the coast of Newfoundland, Canada!

Everything about the physical composition of the leatherback is designed to enhance its ability to live in a marine environment and make adjustments for dramatic changes in pressure and temperature.

These turtles are powerful swimmers and possess a unique physiology that allows their muscles to work at an almost constant rate. Many reptile species completely tire out after even a relatively short burst of physical activity. This reaction is due to the depletion of oxygen levels in the muscles and the increase of lactic acid levels in the blood. Unlike other sea turtles, leatherbacks have a physiology that allows their muscle tissues to remain oxygenated and capable of working for long periods of time. The turtle's large lung capacity is the main reason that they can survive in this manner. In fact, leatherback sea turtles have the capacity for twice the air volume as do green sea turtles.

Scales are present on the fleshy areas of young leatherback sea turtles (Dermochelys coriacea*); the scales are lost as the turtle reaches maturity.*

When female leatherbacks move on land, they do so more efficiently than other sea turtles. Once again, their special physiology proves helpful. Even during the process of laying eggs, the leatherbacks utilize their versatile physiology and breathe with Lamaze-like patterns.

Aside from their special adaptations for enhancing respiration and supplying muscles with oxygen, these turtles also possess an enhanced circulatory system. Their blood has high levels of hemoglobin. Hemoglobin is a protein transported by the red blood cells to the lungs. The hemoglobin then carries the oxygen to the cells in need.

Unlike other turtle species, leatherbacks do not need to bask at the surface between dives. Instead, they maintain a stable body temperature through their low metabolic rate, large body size, and ability to alter their blood circulation. Changing the circulation of the blood is necessary in freezing waters and during dives in freezing temperatures. Blood flow can be restricted from certain parts of the body to maintain a core temperature. Adaptations such as these allow the leatherback to descend to more than 3,000 feet (1,000 meters) up to fifty times a day!

Female leatherbacks have a tail that is smaller than the hind feet. They also feature a considerable suffusion of pink coloration on the head. The pink is due to an increase in blood flow. Males have a concave plastron and a tail that is longer than their hind feet. Males also have a narrower carapace and lack any pink pigmentation on the head.

Leatherback Sea Turtle
Dermochelys coriacea (Linnaeus, 1766)

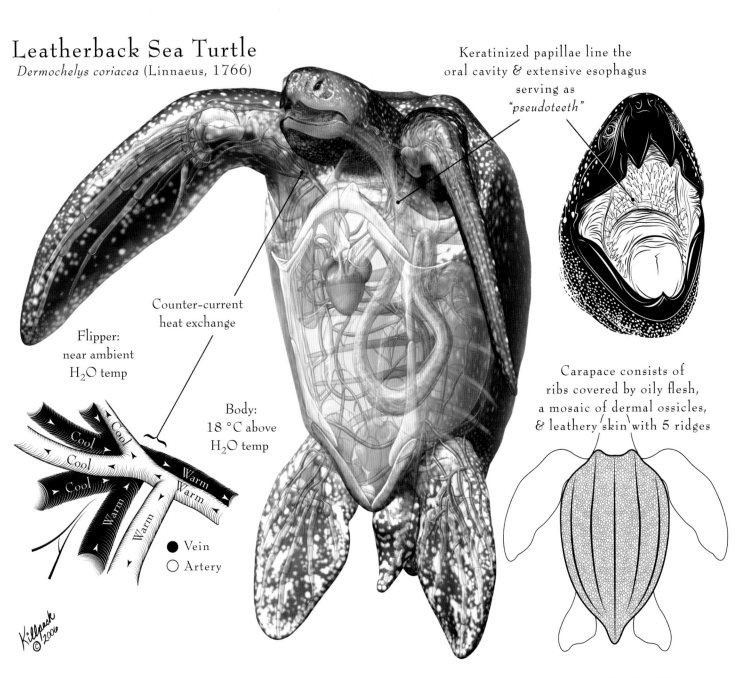

Keratinized papillae line the oral cavity & extensive esophagus serving as *"pseudoteeth"*

Flipper: near ambient H_2O temp

Counter-current heat exchange

Body: 18 °C above H_2O temp

Cool
Cool
Cool
Warm
Warm
Warm
Warm

● Vein
○ Artery

Carapace consists of ribs covered by oily flesh, a mosaic of dermal ossicles, & leathery skin with 5 ridges

David C. Killpack

A pinkish coloration is present on the necks of female leatherbacks; males never come ashore.

Shreyas Krishnan

The reproductive cycle of *D. coriacea* is a well-studied and predictable event. When the time to lay eggs arrives, the female makes her way to the beach. After selecting a desirable location for her nest, she begins the excavation process using her hind flippers. Upon completion of digging the nest, she deposits her eggs. Nesting females emit a range of sounds. Hisses, sighs, and even sounds similar to human belches have been recorded. The female produces 100 to 120 spherical eggs per clutch, six to seven times annually. The incubation period requires fifty to seventy-five days. Upon hatching and emerging from the nest, the young turtles instinctively head toward the water. This event attracts a large number of opportunistic predators, such as birds, mammals, lizards, fish, and crabs. The gauntlet of predators eliminates many hatchlings before and after they enter the water. The high mortality rate faced by hatchlings is counteracted by the large number of eggs that this species produces.

Due to their large proportions, leatherbacks have few natural enemies except for humans. However, at least one specimen fell victim to a natural predator. The turtle was a nesting female in India's Andaman Islands. A herpetologist witnessed the turtle on the beach and saw that it did not move throughout the night. Closer inspection revealed that the turtle was dead. Its hind flipper had been bitten off and the turtle had bled to death. The footprints of a large saltwater crocodile led away from the scene. Over the course of several more days, the crocodile returned to feed upon its feast.

D. coriacea is currently listed as one of the most endangered species by the Convention of International Trade of Endangered Species Act. It is also listed as endangered by the International Union for the Conservation of Nature and Natural Resources (IUCN). The grave reality concerning this species is that it seems to be on an irreversible path toward extinction. Surveys conducted in 1995 revealed between 26,000 and 42,000 nesting females worldwide. These numbers were considerably fewer than the 1980 estimate of 115,000 nesting leatherbacks.

Maintaining this species in captivity long-term is currently beyond the scope of modern zoological institutions. One of the many factors challenging their suitability in captivity is that leatherbacks remain in almost constant motion. Hatchlings continuously swim against the sides of their enclosure and pause only when offered food.

This species is extremely sensitive to human activities and people are completely responsible for its endangered status in the wild. Current leatherback populations cannot tolerate any further pressures without going extinct. We should all endeavor to witness the ancient cycle of sea turtles returning to land in order to nest while we still can and, if possible, help preserve the existence of this fascinating, ancient species.

Researchers are actively documenting the nesting habits and physical characteristics of leatherbacks in an attempt to learn what we can of this fascinating creature before it is too late.

Shreyas Krishnan

Herpetologist Shreyas Krishnan inspects and marks the eggs of olive ridley sea turtles on the Andaman Islands. The eggs were removed from the beach and placed in a protected beachfront hatchery. In their new location, the turtles hatched without the danger of terrestrial and airborne predators.

Shreyas Krishnan

Hidden-Necked Turtles   95

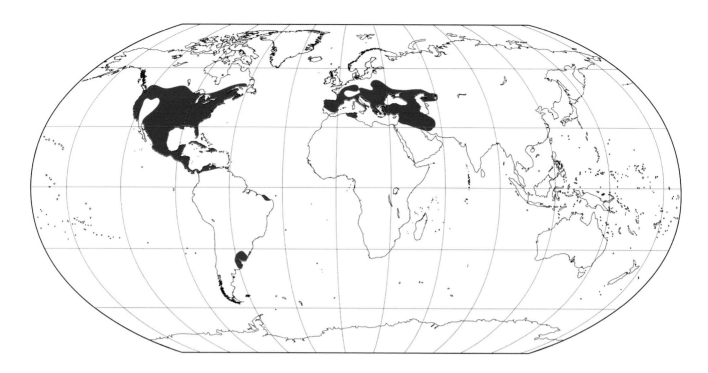

Family Emydidae

Aquatic and Terrestrial Turtles

Represented by eleven genera and forty-one species, the family Emydidae has a natural range that includes Europe to the Aral Mountains of Russia, and North America southward to northeastern Brazil. However, the range of Emydid turtles has been expanding. This increase in geographic distribution is most commonly associated with red-eared sliders (*Trachemys scripta elegans*). Millions of these turtles are bred annually for the pet industry. While United States law prohibits the sale of turtles that have a carapace under 4 inches (10 centimeters) in the pet trade, this law is not present in several other nations. Subsequently, the release of many unwanted pet turtles has caused them to become established in non-native environments.

Emydidae are moderately sized turtles that range in length from the 4-inch (11-centimeter) bog turtle (*Clemmys muhlenbergii*) to the 15-inch (40-centimeter) river cooter (*Pseudemys concinna*). These turtles have oblong or oval-shaped shells with a relatively flattened carapace; however, box turtles (*Terrapene* spp.) possess a domed carapace. Three genera (*Emys, Emydoidea,* and *Terrapene*) have a hinged plastron that allows partial to complete closure of the shell.

Within the family, there are two subfamilies: Emydinae and Deirochelyinae. A generalized distinction between the two groups is that Emydinae is represented by some species that lead at least a semiterrestrial existence or possess a plastral hinge. On the other hand, Deirochelyinae is chiefly aquatic and possesses no such hinge. Emydid turtles are known from fossil records that date back to the Cretaceous period 144 million to 65 million years ago.

Subfamily Emydinae

The spotted turtle (*Clemmys guttata*) is a resident of the wetlands extending from southeastern Canada westward to the Great Lakes basin to northeastern Florida. This small turtle is easily distinguished by its dark shell that bears small yellow spots.

Spotted turtles inhabit bogs, swamps, sphagnum moss seepages, and slow-moving streams. This species prefers a body of clear water with a muddy or soft bottom. Habitat loss has contributed significantly to the decline of the species, as has collection for the pet trade.

Another denizen of swampy areas is the aptly named bog turtle (*Clemmys muhlenbergii*). This species is the smallest of the family Emydidae and the record

Untold thousands of box turtles (Terrapene spp.) have been taken from the wild for sale in the pet trade, causing a dramatic decline in box turtle populations throughout most of their range in the United States.

size for adults is only 4 inches (11 centimeters). Habitat loss from drained wetlands and collection for the pet trade are the greatest factors that threaten the survival of this species. Although protected by law, this species is still highly sought and commands high prices from unscrupulous dealers.

These little turtles have a habitat preference similar to that of the spotted turtle, and when faced with a dangerous situation, they either dive into the water or remain motionless. Given their drab coloration and habit of remaining partially concealed in vegetation when inactive, these turtles are effective at blending in with their surroundings.

The North American wood turtle (*Glyptemys insculpta*) has a historic range that includes the northeastern United States and southeastern Canada. Unlike its congener the bog turtle, the wood turtle prefers habitats such as stream drainages that have hard sand or sand-gravel bottoms. It tends to avoid soft clay-based or mucky bottoms.

Wood turtles demonstrate an inquisitive nature and an acute awareness of their surroundings. The intelligence of this species was tested in a series of maze experiments. Remarkably, the wood turtles learned their way out of the mazes just as quickly as laboratory rats.

Some populations of wood turtle perform an unusual act known as "worm stomping" to obtain food. The hungry turtle stomps its feet and sometimes its plastron several times onto the ground at a rate of about one stomp per second. This act sometimes lasts as long as fifteen minutes. Research has revealed that worm stomping yields an average of 2.4 worms per hour.

The Blanding's turtle (*Emydoidea blandingii*) is found in the Great Lakes region of Canada and the United States, west to Nebraska, with a disjunct population in southern New York and Nova Scotia. Blanding's turtles have a domed carapace with a base coloration that varies from dark brown to black. A series of lightly colored spots accents the dark carapace. The yellowish plastron bears a moveable hinge that allows for partial closure of the shell. One curious distinction is the seemingly permanent smile caused by a notch in the upper jaw.

Blanding's turtles inhabit bodies of shallow water that have abundant shoreline vegetation, such as lakes, ponds, marshes, and coves. When threatened on land, some Blanding's turtles withdraw into the shell and close the plastral hinge. However, the amount of flexibility demonstrated by this hinge varies between populations. Some populations never

*Box turtles, such as this male Mexican box turtle (*Terrapene carolina mexicana*) from northeastern Mexico, often display outlandish colors.*

demonstrate any usage of the hinge; when frightened, these individuals instead try to escape or hide themselves beneath the mud, silt, or other substratum.

Geographically speaking, the pond turtles of North America (*Actinemys* spp.) and Europe (*Emys* spp.) present an interesting situation in that they are closely related but occur on different continents. The Pacific pond turtle (*Actinemys marmorata*) has a historic range that included southern British Colombia (where they have since become extirpated); southward along the Pacific region of Washington, Oregon, extreme western Nevada, and California; and northern Baja California, Mexico. The European pond tur-

tle (*Emys orbicularis*) has a range that includes northern Africa from Tunisia to Morocco; Europe; northern Iran; and near the Aral Sea in Russia. Despite inhabiting two different continents that are separated by an ocean, these species are closely related.

One of the characteristics that differentiate turtles of the family Emydidae from the subfamilies of Emydinae and Deirochelyinae is a hinged plastron. Five species of emydid turtles possess a hinged plastron.

North American box turtles belonging to the genus *Terrapene* are represented by four species. Most of their range lies within the United States from east of the Rocky Mountains and reaching as far west as

Although ornate box turtles (Terrapene ornata) *are a terrestrial species, they are sometimes found enjoying a soak.*

David C. Killpack

*The Mexican spotted box turtle (*Terrapene nelsoni*) is found along the west coast of Mexico. This poorly known species is represented in museums by only a few specimens.*

southeastern Arizona. Box turtles also occur in Mexico, where there are four separate populations.

The common box turtle (*T. carolina*) has a wide distribution and is represented by four subspecies in the eastern United States (one reaches southern Ontario, Canada) and two additional subspecies in eastern Mexico.

The ornate box turtle (*T. ornata*) occupies much of the central United States with a range that extends southwestward into southeastern Arizona and northern Juarez, Mexico. In the eastern limits of their range, ornate box turtles reach from Indiana to Louisiana.

The most endangered species of box turtle is endemic to Mexico. Found only in the marshes of Cuatro Cienegas, Coahuila, Mexico, the Coahuilan box turtle (*T. coahuila*) is the most aquatic of all box turtles.

A species of box turtles that rarely receives much attention is the Mexican spotted box turtle (*T. nelsoni*). No known zoological specimens of this species exist in captivity. Ranging from southern Sonora to Nayarit, Mexico, the spotted box turtle inhabits hill country that is characterized by savanna, oak woodlands, and dry forest scrub.

Subfamily Deirochelyinae

The painted turtle (*Chrysemys picta*), represented by four species, has a widespread distribution that includes most of the United States, southern Canada, and a small population in Chihuahua, Mexico. Painted turtles are absent throughout Florida, most of Texas, and the southwestern United States.

Painted turtles are easy to observe basking alongside bodies of water. These turtles prefer a slow-moving, permanent body of water that has a soft bottom and abundant aquatic vegetation. This species is resistant to the cold and turtles have been seen swimming beneath the ice of frozen ponds on winter days.

Twelve species of map turtles that belong to the genus *Graptemys* inhabit many fast-moving rivers of the eastern United States and southeastern Canada. Despite the broad range of map turtles, most occur only in specific locations on certain river drainages.

The meandering lines on the scutes of these turtles sometimes resemble the contour lines on a map, affording the genus its common name. Map turtles are arguably the most beautiful of the North American turtles. The carapace of many map turtles has a keel. Some species bear projections on the keel, which gives them a saw-backed profile.

*Map turtles, such as this ringed map turtle (*Graptemys oculifera*), are strong swimmers that inhabit fast-moving rivers.*

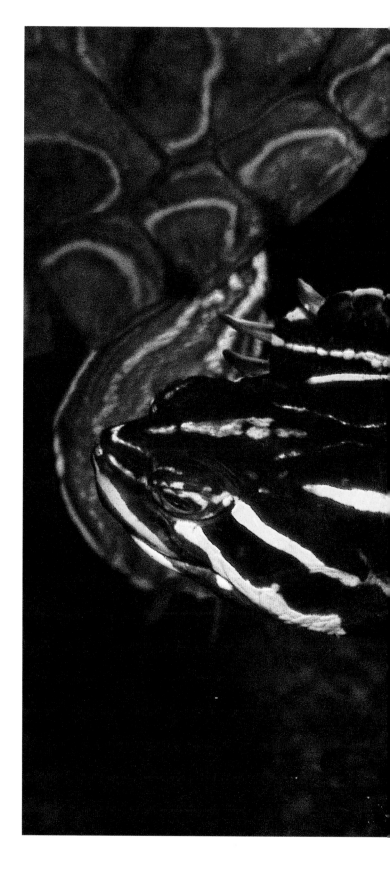

*A pair of Florida red-bellied cooters (*Pseudemys nelsoni*) swim together prior to mating.*

*Some sliders, such as this South American specimen, are at risk of extinction from hybridization with released pet red-eared sliders (*Trachemys scripta elegans*). Unwanted pet turtles should never be released into the wild.*

Juvenile map turtles have brightly colored shells that often feature spike-like projections extending medially from each vertebral scute. The result is a shell with a profile similar to a circular saw blade. When the turtle reaches maturity, the bright colors fade and the projected scutes become reduced or absent. This change is most noticeable among female specimens; upon reaching maturity, they display a prominence of melanin and darkened tones.

Map turtles consume a variety of prey items including mollusks, aquatic arthropods, worms, fish, and amphibians. However, many adult specimens become specialized to eat a diet consisting of freshwater mussels. Many mature females demonstrate macrocephaly, in which the size of the head increases to accommodate the enlarged musculature required for consuming these hard-shelled delicacies.

The diamondback terrapin (*Malaclemys terrapin*) is another mollusk-eating Emydid turtle. It is found along the Atlantic coastline from Cape Cod, Massachusetts, to the gulf coast of south Texas. Unlike other emydids, *Malaclemys* is well suited for the physiological challenges of a life in salt water. Diamondback terrapins occur in tidal creeks, estuaries, and coastal salt marshes.

The diamondback terrapin has been the most popular edible turtle in the history of the United States. When properly cooked, its meat rates highly among the gourmet standard. However, the very reason this turtle became popular is the same reason it is not eaten today. Since so many diamondback terrapins were eaten in the past, they are now rare throughout most of their range.

Aside from the fact that juveniles spend the first years of life drifting among flotsam and floating mats of vegetation, much of this species' ecology and natural history remains a mystery and warrants further research.

The chicken turtle (*Deirochelys reticularia*) of the southeastern United States is another distinctive Emydid. From a distance, it appears similar to a slider or cooter. However, the carapace is notably domed and significantly higher than that of other aquatic emydids.

Of all the turtles in the family Emydidae, chicken turtles have the longest necks. However, this characteristic is not visibly apparent among frightened specimens. Instead, the domed carapace and stripes located on the thighs of this turtle are its identifying marks. The markings on the back of the thighs give the turtle the appearance of wearing striped pants.

Inhabiting the eastern United States to southeastern New Mexico to Coahuila, Nuevo Leon, and Tamaulipas, Mexico, seven species of freshwater turtles of the genus *Pseudemys* are collectively referred to

A strong reliance on good instinct and physical fitness are essential for turtle hatchlings to meet the unforgiving rigors of survival.

as cooters. Attaining a maximum carapace length of 16 inches (40 centimeters), cooters comprise the largest of the emydid turtles.

African slaves coined the term "cooter" in the eighteenth century. The slaves referred to the freshwater turtles by the Bambara or Malinké word *kuta*, which means "turtle." Turtle meat was often included as a menu item for the slaves and the phonetics of the word remains with us today.

The most familiar species of emydid turtle are the sliders (*Trachemys* spp.), which have been introduced globally via the pet trade. Seven species of *Trachemys* are recognized. Sliders have a natural range that includes most of North America, Mexico, Central America, the West Indies, and South America to Argentina. Due to the pet trade, the red-eared slider (*T. scripta elegans*) is now the most familiar introduced species of freshwater turtle.

The release of this species into non-native environments hinders the success of other native species and compromises the natural ecology of those species. The release of pet red-eared sliders into the wild also challenges the ability of native slider populations to maintain their genetic distinction. Unfortunately, unique species and subspecies of the slider have interbred with the common red-eared slider in numerous places, resulting in hybrids.

Family Geoemydidae
Aquatic and Terrestrial Turtles

Comprising twenty-two genera and sixty-seven species, Geoemydidae is the most diverse family of turtles. In overall appearance, members of this family are similar to members of the family Emydidae. The shell is usually oblong or oval-shaped; depending upon the species, the carapace can be domed or relatively flat. The plastron is large and sometimes hinged. The size of the geoemydines varies as well, with the smallest member of the family, the black-breasted leaf turtle (*Geoemyda spengleri*), attaining a carapace length of 5 inches (13 centimeters) and the sizable Malaysian giant turtle (*Orlitia borneensis*) reaching a carapace length of 31 inches (80 centimeters).

The family Geoemydidae is divided into two subfamilies, the Batagurinae and the Geoemydinae. Both are widely distributed throughout much of Asia. Eleven genera and forty-six species represent the wide-ranging subfamily Geoemydinae, which occurs in southwestern India, southern China, Japan, Vietnam, Malaysia, Myanmar, Borneo, Java, Sumatra, and the Philippine Islands. In the Western hemisphere, representatives of this subfamily occupy a geographic range that includes southern

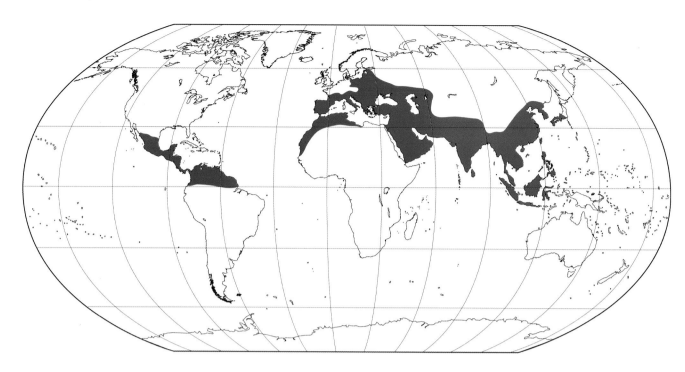

Range of the family Geoemydidae

Mexico and southward through Central America to northern Brazil.

While many members of Geoemydinae are from aquatic margins and some are aquatic, most maintain a terrestrial lifestyle. Of the two subfamilies, the geoemydinae are the smaller, with the largest species attaining a carapace length of 19 inches (48 centimeters).

Nine species represent the genus *Cuora*, otherwise known as Asian box turtles. Like their box turtle counterparts in North America, these turtles have a plastral hinge that can completely close the shell. Depending upon the species, the carapace may have a flattened or domed appearance. *Cuora* have a geographic distribution that includes eastern India, southern Asia, Sulawesi, and the Philippines.

The Southeast Asian box turtle (*C. amboinensis*) is the widest ranging of the species. It occurs from eastern India to Thailand and Vietnam, as well as to the Malay Peninsula and various Indonesian islands including Timor, Sulawesi, and the Moluccas. *C. amboinensis* is found on the Philippines Islands as well.

This small species grows to 8 inches (20 centimeters) in carapace length, has an affinity for life on land, and is a poor swimmer. When found in an aquatic environment, this herbivorous turtle prefers a body of water with a slow current and a soft bottom.

The yellow-headed box turtle (*C. aurocapitata*) is a rare species that historically inhabited a limited range

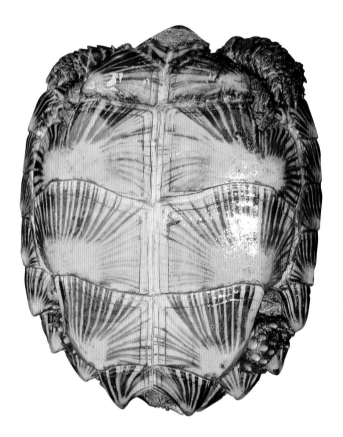

*The plastron of turtles in the family Geoemydidae can be hinged or unhinged as seen in this spiny turtle (*Heosemys spinosa*).*

*Wild populations of the Indochinese box turtle (*Cuora galbinifrons*) of Vietnam and China are facing an uncertain future due to the current trade in Asian turtles.*

*The spot-legged turtle (*Rhinoclemmys punctularia*) of South America is one of the few species of turtles that doesn't normally urinate, defecate, or behave in any offensive manner when picked up.*

*The Indochinese box turtle (*Cuora galbinifrons*) is a shy forest inhabitant that consumes a variety of prey items, including insects, worms, and snails.*

in the Anhui Province of eastern China. Little information exists regarding the natural history or ecology of this species in the wild. Sadly, due to demand from the traditional medicine and pet trades, wild populations of this species may no longer exist.

The yellow-margined box turtle (*C. flavomarginata*) is an omnivorous turtle known to take up residence in rice paddies, ponds, and streams lined with abundant vegetation. Females may lay two clutches per breeding cycle, each consisting of one egg.

Of all the Asian box turtles, the Indochinese box turtle (*C. galbinifrons*) displays the greatest variation in color and shell pattern. This beautiful turtle has a geographic distribution that includes the Tonkin and Annam regions of Vietnam and the southern Guangxi Province and Hainan Island of China.

C. galbinifrons has a highly domed carapace that can grow up to 8 inches (20 centimeters) in length. Although the Indochinese box turtle will enter water, it is the most terrestrial of the *Cuora* and prefers high-elevation forests.

In 1988, a new species of Asian box turtle was discovered and named in honor of Dr. William McCord, a veterinarian and ardent turtle researcher. However, the new species, McCord's box turtle (*C. mccordi*), was acquired from a market and little is known regarding its natural history. The specimen reportedly came from the Guangxi highlands. Although this species may already be extinct in the wild, a small number of captive specimens have produced a modest amount of

offspring. Perhaps the complete extinction of this species will be prevented through captive populations.

Another rare species of *Cuora* is Pan's box turtle (*C. pani*). Described to science in 1984, this turtle is known only from the Yunnan Province of China. Pan's box turtle is critically endangered and fewer than thirty captive specimens constitute our base of knowledge about this rare species.

The Chinese three-striped box turtle (*C. trifasciata*) has an elongated and flattened carapace. The species once had a geographic distribution ranging from northern Vietnam to southeastern China. Unfortunately, this turtle, like many other species of *Cuora*, is facing extinction and can no longer be found throughout much of its former range.

While consumption for food exacts a high toll on most Asian turtles, the Chinese three-striped box turtle is sought mainly for traditional Chinese medicine. It is believed that the shell contains cancer-fighting qualities. Interestingly, chemical evaluations of the shells have found trace amounts of selenium, an element known to protect against cancer. However, these trace amounts are lost due to the modern practices used to render shells into medicinal gel.

C. trifasciata is so rare and valued that the species is sold for $1,000 per kilogram. Specimens in the marketplaces can fetch as much as $3,000. Unfortunately, none of these specimens has been brought to the attention of a herpetologist, despite the promise of significant monetary rewards.

The Yunnan box turtle (*C. yunnanensis*) inhabits high-altitude forests of up to 5,900 feet (1,800 meters) in the Yunnan Province. This species, known only from a few museum specimens, is possibly already extinct in the wild. Another species of Asian box turtle is possibly also extinct in the wild, the Zhou's box turtle (*C. zhoui*). Fortunately for this species, documented captive breeding has occurred.

The keeled box turtle (*Pyxidea mouhotii*) is an Asian box turtle that inhabits India, southern China, and Vietnam. Adults can reach 7 inches (18 centimeters) in carapace length. This turtle possesses a moderately rounded carapace with three longitudinally oriented ridges. The posterior marginal scutes are serrated. A plastral hinge allows the turtle to close the anterior portion of the shell. Reports from wild specimens indicate that this species is herbivorous. However, captive keeled box turtles enthusiastically eat earthworms, soft-bodied insects, and young mice.

Four species represent the Asian leaf turtles of the genus *Cyclemys*. This group of turtles has a geographic distribution that includes northeastern India eastward to Vietnam, the Philippines, and western portions of the Indo-Australian Archipelago. The name *Cyclemys* translates to "circle turtle" and refers to the turtles' round shell. Adults have serrated posterior marginal scutes and a plastral hinge. However, unlike box turtles, the hinge found among *Cyclemys* does not facilitate closing of the shell. Instead, the hinge may play a significant role in assisting females in laying eggs by allowing some outward flexibility of the shell's posterior.

Leaf turtles are commonly associated with forest streams. Hatchlings and juvenile specimens are aquatic, while mature specimens typically lead more of a terrestrial existence.

The striped leaf turtle (*C. atripons*) is the only turtle endemic to the hill country of southeastern Thailand and southwestern Cambodia. The species' common name refers to the darkened bridge that noticeably contrasts the beige plastron. Females achieve a larger size than males and can reach a carapace length of up to 9 inches (22 centimeters). Oldham's leaf turtle (*C. oldhami*) has a range that includes northeastern India, Myanmar, Thailand, and the Malay Peninsula. The stripe-necked leaf turtle (*C. tcheponensis*) has a geographic distribution that includes Vietnam to Thailand. This species can achieve a carapace length of up to 9 inches (22 centimeters). Females deposit ten to fifteen eggs per clutch.

Another group of turtles collectively referred to as leaf turtles include three species belonging to the genus *Geoemyda*. These small turtles reside in tropical forests near water, such as the edges of creeks and streams, and collectively have a range that includes southwestern India eastward to Vietnam, China, and the Japanese island of Okinawa.

The Cochin forest cane turtle (*G. silvatica*) inhabits the midelevation dense evergreen forests of India's Western Ghats. This opportunistic species feeds on fallen ripe fruits, leaves, and a variety of invertebrates.

The Japanese leaf turtle (*G. japonica*) is an endangered species found only on the Ryuku Islands of Japan. Probably the best-known species of *Geoemyda* is the black-breasted leaf turtle (*G. spengleri*), which has the largest geographic distribution for the genus. Its range includes southern China, Vietnam, and Indonesia. This species is omnivorous and resides near water in wooded, mountainous regions.

Four species of semiaquatic forest turtles belonging to the genus *Heosemys* occur in Myanmar to Vietnam, Malaysia including Borneo, Sumatra, Java, and the Philippine Islands. Members of this genus vary considerably in size, from 4 inches (13 centimeters) to 19 inches (48 centimeters) in carapace length.

The Arakan forest turtle (*H. depressa*) attains a carapace length up to 10 inches (25 centimeters). The feet of the Arakan forest turtle suggest that this species maintains a terrestrial existence. Recent investigations in western Myanmar revealed that this turtle is found in shallow streams, near streamside stands of elephant ears, beneath leaf litter, and inside the burrows of pangolins. *H. depressa* consumes a wide range of vegetative matter including fallen fruits, leaves, newly grown stems and shoots, and mushrooms.

The giant Asian pond turtle (*H. grandis*) is the largest member of the genus. Mature specimens reach 19 inches (48 centimeters) in carapace length. Like other members of the genus, *H. grandis* is omnivorous in captivity but predominately herbivorous in the wild. This species is found in ponds, streams, rivers, lakes, swamps, and marshes as well as on land. It has a geographic distribution that includes Myanmar and Vietnam southward to Malaysia.

The Philippine pond turtle (*H. leytensis*) is the rarest member of the genus. It is one of the IUCN's top twenty-five most endangered species. *H. leytensis* historically inhabited only two locations in the Philippines, the Leyte Island and Palauan Island. This species may

be extinct in the wild. Only a few specimens have ever been collected and no additional specimens have been found despite subsequent searches.

Possibly the best known of the *Heosemys* is the spiny turtle (*H. spinosa*). This species occurs in Thailand, southern Myanmar, Malaysia, Indonesia (where it occurs from Kalimantan and various Indonesian islands), and Mindanao Island of the Philippines.

The spiny turtle is at home in mountains and shallow forest streams. This species undergoes a dramatic ontogenetic shift in appearance as it matures. Hatchlings and juveniles possess a spiny shell. Each marginal scute extends at the apex and forms the spines. At the onset of maturity, this feature is obscured. Fully grown specimens show no sign of their former appearance.

Southern Europe, northern Africa, the Middle East, southeastern Asia, and some of the Japanese islands encompass the distribution of the genus *Mauremys*. Seven species represent this genus of semi-aquatic turtles, which inhabit almost every type of body of fresh water including brackish marshes.

In general, *Mauremys* are omnivores that consume aquatic vegetation, fruits, a wide range of invertebrates, and small vertebrates including fish and amphibians. Females lay four to nine elongated, brittle-shelled eggs per clutch.

The Malayan flat-shelled turtle (*Notochelys platynota*) is a monotypic species found in Thailand to southern Vietnam, Malaysia, Sumatra, Java, and Borneo. Adults reach 13 inches (33 centimeters) in carapace length and inhabit shallow bodies of water that have abundant vegetation and a soft bottom, such as jungle ponds, swamps, marshes, and streams.

Little information exists regarding the natural history and ecology of the Malayan flat-shelled turtle in the wild. Due to similarities in overall appearance, discerning the differences between males and females is a challenge.

Hatchling and juvenile Malayan flat-shelled turtles are brightly colored. A variety of hues, from lime green to grayish beige to yellow, adorn the carapace, which may come with or without spots. As the turtle approaches maturity, the coloration of the shell, limbs, and head become darker. Once the turtle reaches adulthood, the colors shift again to a lighter tone. At this time, the head and the soft tissue of the neck bear a good amount of whitish coloration. The shell also undergoes an ontogenetic shift. The darkened brown coloration of the sub-adult changes to a shade of horn yellow to light brown in adult specimens.

Notochelys is herbivorous and reportedly consumes a great deal of aquatic vegetation. When this species is handled or frightened, it often retreats within its shell and defecates.

Two species of dark-colored and semiaquatic turtles found in India, Nepal, Bangladesh, Myanmar, and Sri Lanka comprise the genus *Melanochelys*. The

The painted wood turtle (Rhinoclemmys pulcherrima) *is the most colorful of all the Central American turtles.*

tricarinate hill turtle (*M. tricarinata*) occupies the smallest range in the river basins of eastern India, while the more widespread Indian black turtle (*M. trijuga*) has a range that includes India, Nepal, Sri Lanka, and Myanmar.

Both species of *Melanochelys* are opportunistic feeders and reside in or near clean, flowing streams and ponds with abundant vegetation. Females nest throughout the year and produce three to eight eggs annually.

The black marsh turtle (*Siebenrockiella crassicollis*) is a monotypic species that has a geographic distribution that includes southern Vietnam, Thailand, western Myanmar, and much of the Malaysian peninsula. This species reaches a carapace length of up to 8 inches (21 centimeters). The black marsh turtle is fond of stationary bodies of water that have abundant vegetation and a soft bottom such as ponds, marshes, lakes, and swamps. This little turtle can be found patrolling the bottoms for a meal to scavenge. It preys upon worms, insects, crustaceans, fish, and amphibians.

The reproductive season for the black marsh turtle occurs between April and the end of June. During this time, females may lay as many as four clutches of eggs that each contain one or two eggs.

The genus *Sacalia* comprises three species ranging from southern China and Hainan Island southward to northern Laos and Vietnam. Members of this genus are commonly referred to as eyed turtles. This common name stems from paired spots on the back of the head that are visible from above when the turtle extends its neck.

Members of this genus are of modest size and have a carapace length of just over 5 inches (14.3 centimeters). Throughout their range, these little turtles inhabit midelevation woodland streams between 328 and 1,300 feet (100 to 400 meters) above sea level. Males often bear a strong reddish coloration in the iris and in the soft tissue of the body. Females produce two to six elongated, brittle-shelled eggs per clutch.

An exciting discovery in 1995 led to the description of a new and interesting turtle from Indonesia.

*The spotted pond turtle (*Geoclemys hamiltonii*) is a rare species found only in the Ganges and Indus river drainages.*

The Sulawesi forest turtle (*Leucocephalon yuwonoi*) was discovered among a shipment of tropical fish that was destined for the pet trade. Few details regarding its natural history in the wild are known. However, observations of captive specimens indicate that this species leads a semiaquatic lifestyle, is an excellent climber, and prefers to run away from perceived threats instead of withdrawing into its shell.

Mature male Sulawesi forest turtles are more strikingly colored than females, which bear drab olive brown tones. The soft tissue areas near the males' limbs are creamy white and the head is suffused with a creamy yellow color.

Of all the turtles belonging to the family Geoemydidae, only the tropical wood turtles of the genus *Rhinoclemmys* are represented in the Western Hemisphere. This genus comprises nine species of modestly sized turtles that range in carapace length from nearly 8 to 13 inches (20 to 33 centimeters) and are distributed from southern Sonora and Vera Cruz, Mexico, and southward through Central America to northern Ecuador and Brazil. One species also occurs on the island of Trinidad.

These turtles live in semiaquatic, aquatic, and terrestrial environs. Males initiate courtship by sniffing near the female's vent and attempting to mount her from behind. Mating may take place in or out of the water.

The brown wood turtle (*R. annulata*) inhabits the tropical forests of eastern Honduras, southward along eastern Central America to western Colombia and western Ecuador. Throughout its range, this species occurs in a wide range of habitats including pine forests, alongside creeks, rivers, streams, lowland wet tropical forests, swamps, lagoons, and savannas.

The furrowed wood turtle (*R. areolata*) occupies a more restricted range of southern Vera Cruz, Mexico, to the Yucatan Peninsula, Belize, Guatemala, and northwestern Honduras. Although some specimens have been found in and near aquatic environments, this species is primarily terrestrial.

The Maracaibo wood turtle (*R. diademata*) is endemic to the Maracaibo Basin in Venezuela, where it is seen walking on land and is known to inhabit ponds and streams.

The black wood turtle (*R. funerea*) is an inhabitant of ponds, marshes, rivers, streams, and wet forests from extreme southeastern Honduras southward to Panama. The Colombian wood turtle (*R. melanosterna*) is another inhabitant of various freshwater habitats as well as brackish bodies of water. This species has a geographic distribution that includes eastern Panama to northwestern Colombia and northwestern Ecuador. The large-nosed wood turtle (*R. nasuta*) inhabits rivers of western Colombia and northwestern Ecuador.

If a beauty contest were held among the members of the genus *Rhinoclemmys*, the winner would be the brightly colored painted wood turtle (*R. pulcherrima*). The carapace has a base coloration of horn yellow to brown, and sometimes it bears yellow to red eyespots or stripes bordered in black. The head is often similar to the shell in color, and red to orange stripes typically adorn the face. In some individuals, the iris is a brilliant electric blue.

The spot-legged turtle (*R. punctularia*) can be found in the Orinoco and Amazon river basins of Venezuela, the Guianas, and Brazil, as well as Trinidad and Tobago. Within its range, *R. punctularia* occupies all bodies of fresh water as well as savannas and forests. The female lays eggs throughout the year and produces up to two eggs per clutch. She buries the eggs within leaf litter or near exposed portions of tree roots.

Woodland streams of southern China, Hainan Island, and Vietnam provide the necessary habitat for members of the genus *Sacalia*, which are commonly called four-eyed turtles. These small turtles may reach 6 inches (14 centimeters) in carapace length. A pattern of paired eyespots on the back of the head provides them with their common name.

Beal's eyed turtle (*S. bealei*), which occurs in southern China and northern Vietnam, displays two eyespots. The four-eyed turtle (*S. quadriocellata*) is known from Hainan Island, southeastern China, and Vietnam and it possesses four eyespots on the back of its head. The false-eyed turtle (*S. pseudocellata*) occurs only in the Hainan Province of China; currently, investigators are working to determine whether this is a valid species or simply a hybrid.

Subfamily Batagurinae

This group of geoemydid turtles includes eight genera and twenty-one species occurring from eastern Pakistan to China and Southeast Asia. Seven of the eleven Batagurine genera are monotypic. Most of the twenty-one species are aquatic and none possess a plastral hinge.

The monotypic river terrapin (*Batagur baska*), also known as the tuntong, inhabits fresh water as well as brackish and saltwater tidal estuaries lined with mangroves in Peninsular Malaysia, Sumatra, and the Sundarbands of eastern India. This herbivorous species feeds primarily at night on ripened mangrove fruits that have fallen into the water.

Female *B. baska* are larger than the males and attain a respectable length of 24 inches (60 centimeters). Males reach a maximum carapace length of 20 inches (50 centimeters). A unique distinction for this species is the fact that it has only four claws on the front feet instead of five. Another noticeable characteristic is the extensive amount of webbing that is present between the digits and on the smooth carapace).

Both sexes change from their normal olive coloration to almost completely black during the breeding season. After mating, female river terrapins migrate to sandbanks upriver or to a suitable nesting location along the coast. Reaching a nesting site is not always a simple undertaking. Sometimes the turtles must travel 50 to 60 miles (31 to 38 kilometers) upriver before they reach their destination.

After depositing their eggs, the females conceal the nest with sand. The females bury the eggs and tightly pack the sand into the ground by raising and dropping down onto their plastrons. The result of several 40-pound (18-kilogram) terrapins performing this feat is a loud *tun-tonk* noise, thus earning *B. baska* its common name, tuntong. A typical clutch size consists of twenty spherical eggs that require up to seventy days to hatch.

Despite conservation efforts, wild populations of river terrapins continue to decline. Habitat loss—caused by the destruction of beaches, pollution of the water, loss of mangrove wetlands, damming of rivers, and collection for the pet trade—takes a merciless toll. Sadly, this decline has reduced the noisy sound of nesting tuntongs throughout their range to a small number of nocturnal thuds.

The painted terrapin (*Callagur borneoensis*) shares some similarities with the mangrove terrapin. However, *C. borneoensis* possesses five claws on the front feet as well as a noticeably brighter breeding coloration. Females can attain a carapace length of 23 inches (60 centimeters). While the painted terrapin does consume fallen fruits, its diet comprises leaves, other vegetative matter, crustaceans, and mollusks.

In southern and southeastern Asia, including China, Korea, Taiwan, and Japan, three species comprise the genus *Chinemys*. Reaching a maximum carapace length of 9 inches (24 centimeters), these modestly sized turtles are also known as Chinese pond turtles. Members of this genus have three longitudinally oriented ridges that run the length of the carapace.

The semiaquatic red-necked pond turtle (*C. nigricans*) resides in the mountain streams of southern China and northern Vietnam. The Chinese broad-headed pond turtle (*C. megalocephala*) inhabits ponds and streams. This species is endemic to China and found only in the Nanking region. Reeves' turtle (*C. reevesii*) is the most widespread member of the genus. It is distributed throughout China, Korea, Taiwan, and Japan

The spotted pond turtle (*Geoclemys hamiltonii*) is an attractive monotypic species with a geographic distribution that includes the Ganges and Indus river basins in Pakistan, northern India, Nepal, and Bangladesh. *Geoclemys* grows to a respectable size of 14 inches (36 centimeters) and consumes a variety of aquatic prey items including various arthropods, mollusks, fish, and amphibians. Hatchlings are heavily spotted and bear a slightly serrated keel; in adults, the spotting is less prominent and the keel is lost.

Another monotypic species of the subfamily Batagurinae is the crowned river turtle (*Hardella thurjii*). This sizable inhabitant of oxbow lakes, ponds, and slow-moving rivers can grow to 21 inches (53 centimeters). *Hardella* occurs in the river basins of the Brahmaptura, Ganges, and Indus in Pakistan, northern India, and Bangladesh. This species is mostly aquatic and rarely leaves the water. Basking is usually accomplished by floating at the water's surface. This species is herbivorous and consumes fallen fruits and a variety of aquatic vegetation.

Sexual dimorphism in the crowned river turtle is pronounced. Males have a concave plastron and a longer, thicker tail than females. Females are often three times the size of males. This species possesses a bony lung chamber formed by the lateral wall of the carapace. The chamber protects the lungs from the forces of pressure experienced during deep dives.

Known for its gentle disposition, the yellow-headed temple turtle (*Hieremys annandalii*) resides in lowland swamps, where it feeds on aquatic vegetation. Males are larger than females and can achieve a carapace length of 20 inches (50 centimeters). Females produce four to six oblong eggs per clutch.

The name temple turtle comes from the custom of releasing captured specimens into the waterways of temples. This practice stems from the Buddhist belief that saving any form of life can earn merit in the afterlife. Aside from the symbolic gesture, unfortunately, the relocated turtles are not provided with additional assistance and they are left to fend for themselves.

Seven species comprise the genus *Kachuga*, otherwise known as roofed or tent turtles. This group of aquatic, omnivorous turtles received their common name from the keel on their carapace. Roofed turtles range in size from 9 to 20 inches (23 to 50 centimeters).

Most members of this genus inhabit deep, flowing rivers and are well adapted for diving to considerable depths. Like *Hardella*, many of these species have a bony lung chamber that is useful for protecting the lungs during deep dives.

Throughout their range, the roofed turtles have long been exploited for food. Given such, it comes as little surprise that some of these species are endangered with extinction. The Burmese roofed turtle (*Kachuga trivittata*), endemic to Myanmar, is considered the second most endangered turtle species in the world. In 2006, investigators documented only five nests on a 37-mile-long beach; in 2004, there had been fifteen to twenty nests. Currently, investigators are searching for any additional nesting grounds and looking out for the welfare of recently hatched juveniles. With hard work and education of the local people, the Burmese roofed turtle has a chance to survive the twenty-first century.

In the rice paddies, canals, streams, and ponds of Southeast Asia, there is a modestly sized turtle called the Malayan snail-eating turtle (*Malayemys subtrijuga*). This species has a geographic distribution that includes southern Vietnam, Thailand, southern Myanmar, Malaysia, and Java. Females are considerably larger than males and reach up to 8 inches (21 centimeters) in length. As its common name suggests, this turtle demonstrates a culinary preference for snails. However, like many other aquatic turtles, it also opportunistically consumes a variety of prey items including aquatic arthropods, worms, fish, and amphibians.

Two species represent the genus *Morenia*, otherwise known as eyed turtles. These turtles grow up to 8 inches (21 centimeters) in length and are found in habitats such as slow-moving rivers, ponds, and swamps. The

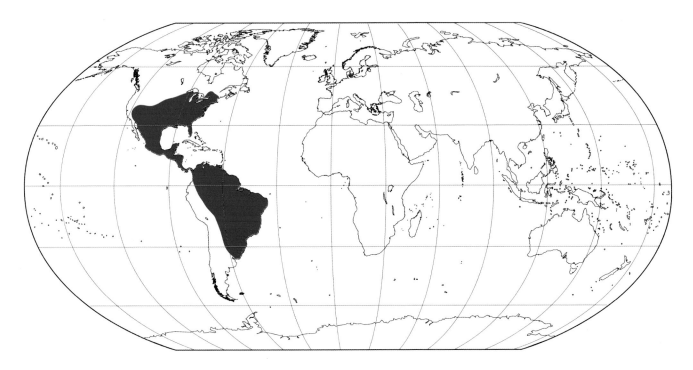

Indian eyed turtle (*M. petersi*) has a geographic range that includes northeastern India and Bangladesh. Its counterpart, the Burmese eyed turtle (*M. ocellata*), is endemic to southern Myanmar.

Family Kinosternidae

Mud and Musk Turtles

The family Kinosternidae consists of two genera and twenty-three species. Four species belong to the genus *Sternotherus* (musk turtles), and nineteen belong to the genus *Kinosternon* (mud turtles). The family Kinosternidae is distributed from southeastern Canada to the United States east of the Rockies and southward to Brazil.

Members of this family are aquatic and sometimes seen patrolling the bottoms of brackish marshes, creeks, flooded fields, lakes, ponds, and rivers. Mud and musk turtles engage in moderate amounts of basking. However, because the turtles' lifestyle causes significant algae growth on their shells, observers occasionally mistake an algae-covered turtle for a rock. Kinosternid turtles are capable of remaining submerged underwater without surfacing for several minutes. Their underwater ability is due in a large part to buccopharyngeal respiration.

Mud and musk turtles have a carapace that is oval-shaped and has twenty-three marginal scutes including the cervical scute. The plastron has ten to eleven scutes and may have a flexible hinge.

As evidenced by fossil material, the family Kinosternidae has been around for a long time. A fossil of *Xenochelys formosa* was discovered in deposits in South Dakota that dated to the Oligocene epoch (23 million to 38 million years ago). This specimen is the oldest known representative of the family.

Musk turtles are small turtles that range in size from 2 to 4 inches (5 to 11 centimeters) in length. Their common name comes from the foul-smelling chemical released when these turtles are frightened or disturbed. Musk glands are located near the bridge and the hind legs.

Musk turtles of the genus *Sternotherus* are only found in North America and have a range that includes southeastern Canada, including Ontario and southern Quebec, and most of the eastern United States from Maine to Wisconsin and south to Texas and Florida.

Musk turtles are surprisingly adept at climbing. They are sometimes found in the branches of trees and against precipitous ledges near the water. This behavior is well documented for the common musk turtle (*S. odoratus*). Should they become startled while

A baby musk turtle withdraws tightly into its shell when handled. Together, the plastron (pictured above) and the carapace (pictured below) provide protection and security. Baby musk turtles are small even when compared to other hatchling turtles.

*The striped mud turtle (*Kinosternon baurii*) is a common inhabitant of aquatic habitats in Florida.*

*The common musk turtle (*Sternotherus odoratus*) can sometimes be found basking in the branches of trees overhanging water.*

perched, the little turtles may drop from these locations—which can cause a fair amount of alarm for someone venturing too near. Sometimes fishermen become unwitting victims to a frightened musk turtle that falls into their boat or on the top of their heads!

Comprising nineteen species, mud turtles of the genus *Kinosternon* represent a majority of the turtle diversity within the family Kinosternidae. Of the twenty-five species belonging to the family, there are sixteen that occur in Latin America. Six species are endemic to the United States, at least seven are endemic to Mexico, and one species occurs only in Colombia.

Family Platysternidae

The Big-Headed Turtle

The big-headed turtle (*Platysternon megacephalum*) is the only living member of the family Platysternidae. *Platysternon* is a moderately sized turtle that attains a carapace length of up to 7.25 inches (18.4 centimeters). It has a range that includes southeastern China, including Hainan Island, Mynamar, Thailand, and Vietnam. Throughout its range, five subspecies exist: *P. m. megacephalum*, the Chinese big-headed turtle of southern China; *P. m. peguense*, the Burma big-headed turtle of southern Myanmar to southern Thailand; *P. m. shiui*, the Vietnam big-headed turtle of Langson Province in north Vietnam; *P. m. tristernalis*, the Yunnan big-headed turtle of the Mekong River basins of the Yunnan Province, China; and *P. m. vogeli*, the Thailand big-headed turtle of northwest Thailand.

Big-headed turtles typically have an olive to dark brown carapace. The posterior margin of its carapace is noticeably wider than the anterior portion, due to the outwardly flaring posterior marginal scutes. The species' common name is derived from the turtle's massive triangular head, which is so large that it cannot completely withdraw into the shell. The head is arguably the most distinctive characteristic possessed by this species. However, the hooked jaw, long tail, and reduced plastron are also undeniably distinctive.

The big-headed turtle's fleshy inguinal areas bear numerous tubercles. The tail is almost as long as the carapace and covered with large scales. Large scales also cover the front portions of the forelimbs. Well-developed claws are present on the tips of the webbed feet. Many specimens have orange coloration on the fleshy areas of their bodies, including small orange spots on the sides of the head. Young specimens are

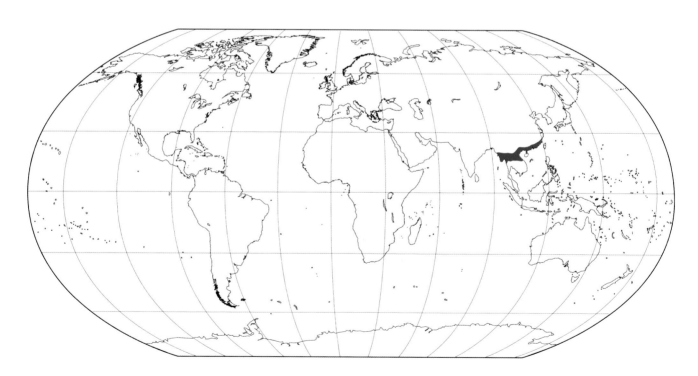

Range of the family Platysternidae

*The big-headed turtle (*Platysternon megacephalum*) inhabits rocky mountain streams and is active mainly at night.*

The big-headed turtle uses its strong tail to help support its body while climbing slippery rocks

more brilliantly marked and the rim of the carapace is serrated.

The big-headed turtle inhabits cool, fast-moving rivers and steep, cascading mountain streams. The sharp claws and muscular tail help the turtle climb and negotiate its slippery, rocky environs. During the day, big-headed turtles remain inactive and hide beneath overhanging ledges, or burrow into gravel or under a rock at the bottom of a streambed. During the night, these turtles actively patrol the streams for food or mates. Occasionally, big-headed turtles are found amid the branches and low shrubs overhanging the water.

Males are distinguished from females by the presence of a large tail with a cloacal opening that extends just beyond the rim of the carapace. Our understanding of juveniles comes primarily from data obtained from wild specimens; only a few reproductive events have occurred in captivity. Much of this species' natural history remains shrouded in mystery and warrants further study.

Family Staurotypidae

Giant Musk Turtles

Turtles belonging to the family Staurotypidae are the largest of the musk turtles. The Mexican giant musk turtle (*Staurotypus triporcatus*) can grow to 15.7 inches (40 centimeters) in carapace length. This family is represented by two genera and three species. The

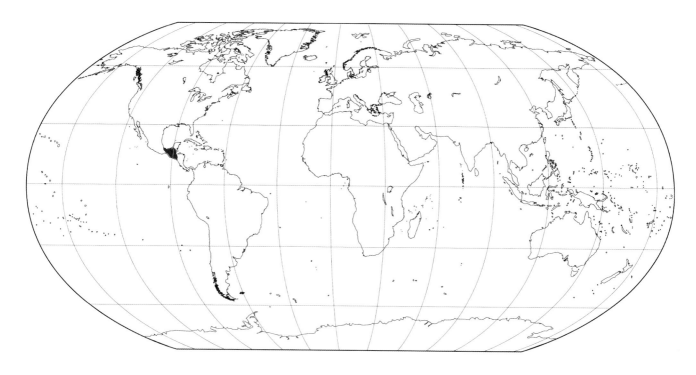

Range of the family Staurotypidae

turtles have a range that includes southern Mexico to northern Honduras.

All turtles belonging to the family Staurotypidae possess a cross-shaped plastron and powerful jaws that are complete with thick, curved cusps. Unlike many turtle species, the sex of their offspring is not temperature dependent; instead, it is determined by chromosomes.

The genus *Staurotypus* is represented by two species; the genus *Claudius* is represented by a single monotypic species. The narrow-bridged musk turtle (*Claudius angustatus*) is the smallest member of the family with adults reaching 6.5 inches (16.5 centimeters) in length. *Claudius* is also the only species of turtle that possesses a sharp cusp below

*Unlike other turtles, the keels on the shell of the Mexican giant musk turtle (*Staurotypus triporcatus*) become more prominent as the turtle matures.*

The narrow-bridged mud turtle (Claudius angustatus) of Central America has a perfectly designed cusp for eating frogs and other slippery prey items.

the eye on either side of the jaw. The cusp, combined with a sharply hooked lower jaw, is useful in securing slippery and wriggling prey such as tadpoles and frogs.

The ferocity of the Mexican giant musk turtle, called the guao by the Mayans, is legendary. During his investigations of the amphibians and reptiles of Central America, noted nineteenth-century herpetologist Edward Drinker Cope recorded a tale depicting just how brutal the guao's struggle for life can be. Indians informed the biologist of an alligator (possibly a Morelett's crocodile) that had swallowed a guao. Although this aspect of the story was not unique, the fact that the turtle chewed itself out of the crocodilian's stomach will live in infamy.

Family Testudinidae

Tortoises

With their club-like feet that are reminiscent of pachyderms, their slow and deliberate demeanor, and their preference for living on dry land, tortoises epitomize the terrestrial turtle. The family Testudinidae, the third most diverse family of chelonians, is represented on five different continents. Currently, the family Testudinidae includes thirteen genera and fifty

species. At least 80 percent of tortoise diversity occurs in the southern latitudes including Africa, Madagascar, India, Southeast Asia, South America, the Seycehelles Islands, and the Galápagos Islands. The remaining portion of tortoise diversity lies within the southern United States, Mexico, southern Europe, and western Asia.

Like many other groups of turtles, tortoises occupied a greater range during earlier times. Fossil evidence of tortoises comes from Eocene deposits some 55 million to 34 million years ago. During this time, tortoises lived in northern Europe, Central Asia, and throughout most of North America including southern Canada as well as the West Indies. However, older fossils in Mongolia date back to the late Paleocene epoch and indicate that these reptiles first appeared some 56 million years ago.

Tortoises possess distinctive physical characteristics that differentiate them from other chelonians. Their sturdy feet lack webbing, and the number of bones at the tip of the digits are absent or greatly reduced in number. These characteristics help the tortoise support its heavy, sometimes bulky, body on land.

The stereotype of tortoise morphology is a highly domed shell. However, this characteristic is not a standard criterion for belonging to the family

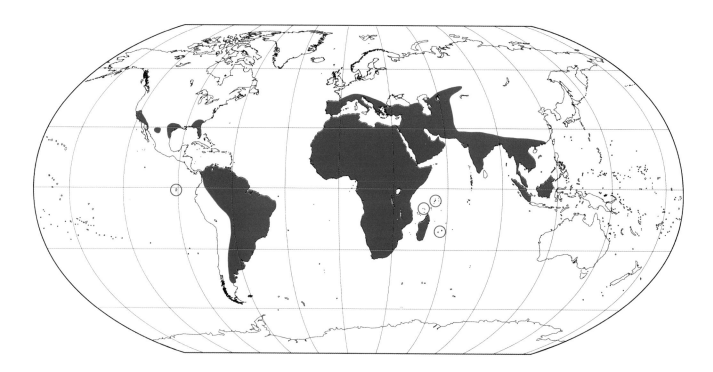

Testudinidae. Interestingly, tortoises demonstrate a diverse range of physical characteristics that are designed to enhance their survival in nature.

From flat shells to domed shells to elongated shells with posterior-oriented hinges, tortoises come in a variety of shapes and sizes. Some of the smallest and largest turtles in the world are tortoises. The speckled padlopers (*Homopus signatus*) of South Africa measure a mere 4 inches (10 centimeters) when full grown, while the Aldabra giant tortoises (*Dipsochelys dussumieri*) of the Aldabra Atoll in the Seychelles Islands grow to incredible lengths of 49 inches (125 centimeters) and weigh in excess of 550 pounds (250 kilograms)!

Given the wide geographic range of tortoises, it comes as no surprise that they also inhabit a wide range of habitats including deserts, savannas, prairies, tropical rainforests, rocky crevices, volcanic islands, and high-altitude tropical forests.

Three genera and six species of Indo-Asian tortoises occur in India, Sri Lanka, Nepal, Myanmar, Thailand, Vietnam, Malaysia, Indonesia, Borneo, and China. Throughout their range, the Indo-Asian tortoises occur in lowland tropical rainforests, grassy fields, and evergreen mountain forests up to 6,600 feet (2,000 meters) in elevation.

The Indo-Asian tortoises pose a dilemma to scientists and conservationists alike. These tortoises inhabit areas where exploitation and habitat loss occurs at an alarming rate. Therefore, the biology and ecology of these species remain shrouded in mystery.

Within the Indo-Asian region, the genus *Geochelone* occurs in India, Pakistan, Nepal, and southern Myanmar. The two species found in this range are the Indian star tortoise (*G. elegans*) and the Burmese star tortoise (*G. platynota*). The Indian star tortoise resides in dry grasslands and tropical deciduous forests. Its eastern counterpart, the Burmese star tortoise, leads an imperiled existence in the tropical dry forests of southern Myanmar.

Residing within the forested regions of eastern India, Vietnam, China, Sumatra, and Borneo are two species of tortoise that belong to the genus *Manouria*. The Asian brown tortoise (*M. emys*) can be found in well-drained evergreen rainforests up to 3,300 feet (1,000 meters) in elevation. This tortoise attains a length of up to 20 inches (50 centimeters) and occupies a range that includes eastern India to Vietnam, Malaysia, Sumatra, and Borneo. The rare impressed tortoise (*M. impressa*) inhabits the hillsides of evergreen tropical mountain forests at elevations of 3,300 to 6,600 feet (1,000 to 2,000 meters). When fully grown, this tortoise reaches 12 inches (30 centimeters) in length and occupies a range that includes Myanmar and Malaysia to Vietnam and China.

*The impressed tortoise (*Manouria impressa*) is a forest dweller that feeds almost entirely on mushrooms.*

The Asian tortoises of the genus *Indotestudo* have a geographic distribution that extends from western India eastward to Guangxi, China, and south to Indonesia. Specimens can achieve a carapace length of up to 14 inches (36 centimeters). The Asian tortoises have a flattened and elongated carapace that has descending sides. *Indotestudo* are creamy beige with dark blotches of various shading and size on the carapace, legs, neck, and head.

Asian tortoises undergo a slight color change during the breeding season, with both sexes displaying a reddish coloration around the nostrils and the eyes. This coloration is more brilliant among the males than among the females. The sexes can also be differentiated by their size because males are larger than females. Females lay up to four eggs per clutch.

Asian tortoises are primarily herbivorous and they consume fruits, flowers, and fungi. However, there have been reports of some tortoises that consume slugs. Males are known to vocalize during rainstorms occasionally.

With seven genera and twenty-one species distributed throughout the continent, Africa is the cradle of tortoise diversity. A partial explanation for such a richness in species is the continent's diverse ecological zones. Not only do more different types of tortoises live in Africa than anywhere else, but they also demonstrate adaptations to the continent's various ecological zones.

The four species belonging to the genus *Testudo* occupy a range along Africa's northern desert and Mediterranean coast. The African spurred tortoise (*Geochelone sulcata*) inhabits the lowland, sub-arid desert of central Africa from Mauritania and Senegal to Ethiopia. The largest of the continental tortoises, these chelonians can attain a maximum shell length

*In some parts of its range, the Central Asian tortoise (*Testudo horsfieldii*) spends up to six months hibernating below ground.*

The African pancake tortoise (Malacochersus tornierii*) earned its common name from its flattened shell.*

of 30 inches (76 centimeters) and a weight of 180 pounds (82 kilograms). African spurred tortoises occupy one of the hottest and driest regions in Africa.

The second-largest species of African tortoise, the leopard tortoise (*Geochelone pardalis*), occupies a wide range in Africa that extends from Sudan to Angola and southward to the Republic of South Africa. Depending upon the subspecies or population examined, shell lengths for adults reach upward of 18 inches (45 centimeters) and a well-fed adult can weigh as much as 80 pounds (36 kilograms).

From Senegal to Ethiopia and southward to Botswana and the Republic of South Africa lies the distribution range of six species of medium-sized tortoises of the genus *Kinyxis*, commonly referred to as the hinge-back tortoises. These tortoises occupy a variety of habitat types and, depending upon the species, are found in grassy savannas, tropical rainforests, swamps, forest margins, and dry scrub forests. The most notable characteristic of these tortoises is a moveable hinge on the posterior of the carapace. In fact, *Kinyxis* is the only group of turtles that has a hinge in this location. When

the tortoise perceives danger, it tightly closes the posterior portion of its shell while protecting its head with tightly pressed forelimbs.

Hinge-back tortoises are omnivorous and consume a wide range of fruits, plants, fungi, and invertebrates such as snails, worms, and arthropods.

Of all the hinge-back tortoises, one species lives a lifestyle unique to the primarily terrestrial tortoise. The serrated hinge-back tortoise (*K. erosa*) lives a semiaquatic lifestyle in or near the swamps and rivers within wet, tropical rainforests in western Africa. A testament to its aquatic preferences, *K. erosa* is a capable swimmer.

Among the boulder-strewn arid scrub habitats of Kenya and Tanzania, there resides a most interesting monotypic species of tortoise. Unlike any other tortoise in the world, the African pancake tortoise (*Malacochersus tornieri*) possesses a light, flexible shell that is almost completely flattened.

Pancake tortoises prefer to reside in rocky outcrops. Such locations are perfectly suited for this species. Due to the low profile of its shell, *Malacochersus* is able to escape into the cracks and crevices between boulders upon the first sign of danger. Once securely situated within a far recess, the tortoise positions its limbs so that removing it from the hiding place becomes impossible. Pancake tortoises, quick and agile compared to other terrestrial chelonians, move nimbly within the rocky habitat.

Three genera and six species of tortoises are endemic to the Cape region of South Africa. The South African bowsprit tortoise (*Chersina angulata*) is a monotypic species, although this small tortoise is possibly a distant relative of the hinge-back tortoises.

The two remaining genera of tortoises in this region are the padlopers (*Homopus* spp.) and the South African star tortoises (*Psammobates* spp.). *Homopus* is represented by five species of small tortoises, the largest of which attains a maximum length in excess of 6 inches (16 centimeters). *Homopus* includes the smallest species of tortoise in the world, the speckled padloper.

The genus *Psammobates* includes three species. The carapacial scutes of these small and beautiful tortoises are centrally raised to form a knob. Light and dark bands arranged in a radial fashion provide a striking geometric pattern, thus affording the common name geometric tortoise. Like the other South African endemics, these tortoises are endangered. Fortunately, there are organizations dedicated to the conservation and research of these fascinating tortoises.

Interestingly, the world's largest species of tortoises are found only on small islands. Fossils of giant tortoises from North America, South America, and Africa indicate that these behemoths once occupied a much wider distribution.

Some 650 miles (1,045 kilometers) off the coast of Ecuador and isolated in the Pacific Ocean lie the Galápagos Islands. These volcanic islands have never been inhabited by aboriginal tribes and are so remote that they have only been known to humankind for approximately four hundred years. Since their discovery, the Galápagos Islands have become famous for their rare, distinctive variety of animals.

Once discovered, the Galápagos Islands attracted the attention of seafaring whaling vessels in need of food. The giant tortoises of the Galápagos (*Geochelone nigra*) were a conspicuous sight and they soon became a replenishing supply of food for crewmembers at sea. As with the giant tortoises of the Seychelles Islands, the tortoises of the Galápagos were loaded into ships. Often, hundreds at a time were taken aboard, where they could survive for several months without food or water. Since the ships had no means of refrigeration, this food source was ideal for the sailors. The slaughter of these tortoises for food continued until the 1950s.

It was on the Galápagos Islands, amid the fascinating biota, that Charles Darwin synthesized his theories about natural selection. The following is an excerpt from Darwin's *Voyage of the Beagle*:

The day was glowing hot and the scrambling over the rough surface and through the intricate thickets, was very fatiguing; but I was well repaid by the strange Cyclopean scene. As I was walking along I met two large tortoises, each of which must have weighed at least two hundred pounds: one was eating a piece of cactus, and as I approached, it stared at me and slowly walked away; the other gave a deep hiss, and drew in its head. These huge reptiles, surrounded by the black lava, the leafless shrubs, and large cacti, seemed to my fancy like some antediluvian animals. . . . The breast-plate roasted, with the flesh on it, is very good; and the young tortoises make excellent soup; but otherwise the meat to my taste is indifferent.

Today it is unlikely that anyone can relate to Darwin's experience of consuming tortoise flesh beyond reading his description of the meal. Strict conservation regulations were set for the Galápagos Islands during the early 1950s. The prohibition of taking or killing the tortoises was necessary to prevent the imminent extinction of this incredible species.

At one time, fifteen distinct subspecies of Galápagos tortoises existed on the separate islands. These populations were decimated—not only by humans, but by predation from rats, cats, and ferocious feral dogs brought to the islands. In addition, the arrival of goats and other grazers ruined the tortoises' once pristine habitat. Today, only thirteen subspecies exist. Of these surviving subspecies, one is almost extinct. The giant tortoise of Pinta Island (*G. n. abingdoni*) maintains a tenuous hold on existence with one surviving male. Lonesome George is the last of his kind and is currently maintained under secure captive conditions at the Charles Darwin Research Center on Santa Cruz Island.

Like many other species of fauna occurring on the Galápagos Islands, the Galápagos tortoises from different islands demonstrate morphological adaptations

Giant island-dwelling tortoises, such as this Galápagos tortoise (Geochelone nigra)*, present many interesting questions and ideas about evolutionary concepts.*

that facilitate life under different conditions. The smaller islands do not support the same amount of vegetation as the larger islands; tortoises living on smaller islands are smaller, with males rarely exceeding 120 pounds (54 kilograms). These tortoises also possess a distinctive carapace described as "saddleback." Saddleback carapaces are highly elevated above the neck and flared outward over the hind feet. Tortoises with a saddleback carapace can raise the head vertically to browse on hanging vegetation as well as drop the head for grazing. In fact, the saddle-shaped shells are what inspired early Spanish explorers to name the tortoises and the islands Galápagos. *Galápago* is an old Spanish term for a specific type of saddle with an upturned front.

Male Galápagos tortoises are larger than females and size does matter. When competing for females,

males combat one another by hissing, biting, and ramming into one another's shells. The saddleback varieties also see who can raise their head the highest. When it comes time for mating, the courtship of the Galápagos tortoise is not a gentle event. The male simply overpowers the female by ramming into her side and mounting her. During mating, the male sometimes drops his head down to the female's withdrawn head and emits a bellowing grunt.

Galápagos tortoises consume virtually any vegetative matter they encounter, including the spiny, prickly pear cactus that grows on the islands. However, the introduction of goats onto the island provided the tortoises with a considerable amount of competition for food. Fortunately, a goat eradication program was enacted and the hoofed beasts were summarily removed from the islands.

Small ground finches of the Galápagos Islands remove ticks from Galápagos tortoises (Geochelone nigra). The tortoise solicits this behavior by extending its neck and allowing the finches to scan all the nooks and crannies to find the noxious parasites.

While the islands of the Galápagos have undoubtedly fueled the inspiration of several budding biologists and conservationists, there is another group of islands inhabited by giant tortoises.

In the West Indian Ocean, some 400 miles (250 kilometers) east of the northern coast of Tanzania, are 115 granite- and coral-based islands that compose the Seychelles Islands. When first discovered by Europeans in 1609, these tropical islands hosted six species of giant tortoises. By the 1840s, only three of these species remained.

Sub-fossil materials from the Seychelles, together with Madagascar and the Mascarene Islands, indicate that this region once supported two genera (*Cylindropsis* and *Dipsochelys*) and twelve species of giant tortoises. The sub-fossil remains date from 750 to 2,850 years ago.

All six species belonging to the genus *Cylindropsis* and all but three species of *Dipsochelys* are extinct. No complete skeletal remains of these tortoises have ever been found. However, measurements of shell portions and other bones indicate that these tortoises once reached at least 24 inches (60 centimeters) in carapace length.

During the 1600s, the Seychelles was a known destination for whaling vessels, explorers, and settlers. During this time, the unique tortoises living on the island were killed for meat, gathered by the hundreds as a food source for seafaring vessels, or simply removed. By the 1840s, only the tortoises living on the inhospitable Aldabra Islands, some 700 miles (1,130 kilometers) away from the Seychelles, were alive.

It was also during this time that the first conservation initiative for these creatures was formed. Prominent scientists of the era, including Charles Darwin and Lord Walter Rothschild, appealed for the conservation of the fauna of the Indian Ocean islands.

Although originally confined to the islands of the Aldabra Atoll, the Aldabra giant tortoise (*Dipsochelys dussumieri*), which numbers more than 100,000 in the wild, has been introduced to some of the Seychelles Islands.

The Seychelles Island was originally home to the Seychelles saddle-backed tortoise (*D. arnoldi*), also known as Arnold's tortoise. The island was also the home to the Seychelles giant tortoise (*D. hololissa*). The Seychelles giant tortoise is the largest member of the genus and can attain a straight carapace length of 48 inches (123 centimeters).

However, ships routinely visited the island to fill their hulls with the tortoises that could survive for months at sea without food or water. Once brought aboard, the animals were turned over onto their backs and stacked upon one another until one was needed to feed the crew. By 1840, these giant reptiles had vanished from the islands.

Both of the tortoises that had been native to the Seychelles were believed to be extinct until 1997, when adult specimens were found living in captivity. Currently there are eighteen known adult specimens of *D. arnoldi* and twelve living specimens of *D. hololissa*. Fortunately, the Nature and Protection Trust of the Seychelles is working to safeguard these giants from extinction with an active captive breeding program.

The name *Dipsochelys* translates into "drinking tortoise." These tortoises have a special flap inside the skull that allows them to drink while continuing to breathe. This important survival strategy allows the tortoises to devote as much time as possible to maintaining hydration on a sunny tropical island.

Giant tortoises earn their namesake in every sense of the word. A Galápagos tortoise (*Geochelone nigra*) named Goliath, who has lived at the Life Fellowship Bird Sanctuary in Seffner, Florida, since 1960, possesses a carapace length of 53 inches (21 centimeters), a width of 40 inches (16 centimeters), a height of 27 inches (11 centimeters), and a weight of 849 pounds (350 kilograms).

Giant tortoises are also long-lived. The oldest specimen is a male Aldabra giant tortoise (*Dipsochelys dussumieri*) named Adwaitya that lived at the Kolkata Zoo in India until his death in 2006. British seamen originally brought the tortoise to the zoo as a gift from the Seychelles in 1875. Zoo records estimate that the tortoise hatched in 1750, although some believe it was as early as 1705. These estimates indicate that Adwaitya was either 256 or 301 years old before he succumbed to an infection and died. At the time of this writing, investigators are using carbon dating to help pinpoint the exact age of this tortoise.

In the United States, tortoises are distributed throughout the Southeast, southern Texas, and the Southwest. In Mexico, they exist in northeastern and north-central regions. Beyond these localities, tortoises do not occur until South America, where they are distributed east of the Andes and north of Patagonia.

In North America, the genus *Gopherus* is represented by four species, all of which are endangered.

While this Berlandier's tortoise (Gopherus berlandieri) *made it across an isolated rural road, many others are hit and killed by careless drivers. Berlandier's tortoises are most active and can be found crossing roads in the spring during the morning hours and also after summer thunderstorms.*

Depending upon the species, these modestly sized tortoises range from 8 to 20 inches (20 to 50 centimeters).

Male *Gopherus* are territorial and defend their areas from other males. If another male enters one male's territory, combat ensues. Combating males hiss, ram their gular scutes into their rival's shell, and bite at the legs, face, feet, and carapace of their opponent. The winner of these bouts is determined when one turtle has been overturned and is left struggling to right himself.

The courtship of these tortoises is similar among the species. It often involves the male circling the female and performing head bobs in an attempt to gain her attention. Some males use a more direct approach by circling the female while biting her head, limbs, and shell. The male sometimes even rams into the sides of the female's shell with his gular scute until she withdraws into her shell and remains submissive.

Male and female *Gopherus* possess glands on the undersides of the jaws. The purpose of these glands is not fully understood; however, they do seem to play a role in the transition from courtship to coitus. Females lay up to four eggs per clutch that generally require ninety days of incubation.

The gopher tortoise (*G. polyphemus*) is a modestly sized species with a maximum length of 15 inches (38 centimeters). This burrowing tortoise resides in the sandy prairies and forests of southern South Carolina and throughout most of Florida westward to eastern Louisiana. The burrows these tortoises dig are not only essential to their own survival but to the survival of several other organisms that later use the holes. Fellow burrowers include various species of amphibians, snakes, burrowing owls, and mammals such as opossums, raccoons, and rodents.

Unfortunately, gopher tortoises are facing the possibility of extinction, primarily due to habitat loss. Laws protect the gopher tortoise from collection for the pet trade, but these statutes do little to hinder land developers.

Northeastern New Mexico and southern Texas to Coahuila, Nuevo Leon, and Tamaulipas, Mexico, is the natural range of Berlandier's tortoise (*Gopherus berlandieri*). Measuring up to 8 inches (20 centimeters), this species has a shell that varies in color from tan to dark brown. Individuals that have a dark brown carapace also have a yellowish spot on the center of each carapacial scute.

During the day, Berlandier's tortoise rests on a cushion of vegetation or stays slightly concealed within a scraped-away portion of soil near the base of a shrub or patch of vegetation. After continuous use, these scrapes can increase in depth to 3 feet (1 meter) or more. Some individuals dig a burrow; however, many habitats within the range of *G. berlandieri* consist of dry, rocky soils. In locations such as these, the tortoises utilize previously excavated mammal burrows.

Male Berlandier's tortoises possess a prominent gular scute that has a slightly upwardly curved forked end. This projection is used as a weapon of sorts when combating for reproductive privileges. Should two males encounter a female during the breeding season, combat soon follows. The tortoise uses the scute as a battering ram with the intention of overturning and immobilizing the rival male.

Today, habitat loss and roadway mortality constitute the largest challenges to this species in the wild. Until the late 1960s, large numbers of wild Berlandier's tortoises were taken for sale in the pet trade. Untold thousands of these reptiles died in waiting pens, and untold more perished in the hands of their new owners. Today, the possession of these tortoises is restricted to licensed wildlife rehabilitators and specially permitted institutions.

*Male red-footed tortoises (*Geochelone carbonaria*) use their well developed eyesight to find food as well as female red-footed tortoises. Males of this species are discriminating compared to most male tortoises and only mate with females of their own species.*

The largest member of the genus *Gopherus* is the desert tortoise (*G. agassizii*). Adult specimens can reach up to 20 inches (50 cm) in length and have a distribution in the United States that includes western Arizona, southwestern California, southern Nevada, and southwestern Utah. In Mexico, desert tortoises occur in northwestern Sinaloa, western Sonora, Isla de Tiburon, and northern Baja California.

Besides habitat loss, the pet trade has played a significant role in the desert tortoise's decline. In California and Nevada, an estimated 250,000 specimens are kept as pets. Despite laws declaring the protection of this species, desert tortoises have a long history as a commonly kept species in captivity.

Another crucial factor challenges current populations of desert tortoises. The bacterium *Mycoplasmosis agassizii* causes an upper respiratory tract disease found among certain populations of desert tortoises in the Mojave Desert. The illness often has fatal results, and there is currently no treatment or cure. Symptoms of mycoplasmosis infection include wheezing, neck distention, loss of appetite, and wet discharge of fluids and mucous from the nostrils. Some specimens may not display any symptoms and still

Several species of tortoises are becoming severely endangered in the wild. Fortunately, many zoos have succeeded in breeding some of these rare species, including the radiated tortoise (Geochelone radiata) of Madagascar.

serve as a carrier of the disease. This fact was discovered after lesions were found on the lungs of a seemingly healthy specimen. Specimens that became infected in captivity and were subsequently released may have caused the disease among wild populations.

Desert tortoises are especially adapted for life in the hot and dry desert landscape. However, this environment makes it particularly important that wild specimens not be molested or disturbed. Picking up a tortoise or turtle often causes the animal to release its bladder. Losing moisture via urination in a severe desert environment could be detrimental to the health of the

tortoise. Depending upon the age and size, a female desert tortoise can lay up to nine eggs per clutch.

The bolson tortoise (*G. flavomarginatus*) inhabits the arid grasslands, or bolsons, of north-central Mexico including the Bolson of Mapimi of southeastern Chihuahua, southwestern Coahuila, and northeastern Durango. This species can grow to 16 inches (40 centimeters) in length and has a yellow, straw-colored, or brown carapace. The central portions of the carapacial scutes vary from dark brown to black and the marginals are lighter in color.

Bolson tortoises consume grasses, various plants, the pads and fruits of prickly pear cactus, and occasionally insects. These accomplished burrowers can construct tunnels up to 33 feet (10 meters) in length. The tortoises and other creatures seek refuge in these burrows during times of extreme heat and cold.

Several of the bolsons in north-central Mexico, including the Bolson of Mapimi, have been going through a drying trend. This trend has negatively affected the regional flora, which in turn reduces the amount of food available for the tortoises. Only small populations of bolson tortoises can be found in the wild. Mexican law does protect the bolson tortoise because it is endangered there.

Three species of tortoises occur in South America from southeastern Panama to Colombia, Venezuela, Guyana, French Guiana, Suriname, eastern Brazil, Peru, eastern Bolivia, Paraguay, and northern Argentina. These areas comprise the indigenous range of the red-footed tortoise (*Geochelone carbonaria*). Red-footed tortoises are established on a number of islands, including Trinidad, the Virgin Islands, and several Caribbean islands including Corn Island of Nicaragua.

These beautiful tortoises have bright red markings on the head and large red scales on the anterior portions of the legs and the dorsal surface of the tail. The base coloration of the shell is dark brown to black, and yellow to reddish orange spots are present on the center of the scutes. Adult red-footed tortoises may reach 20 inches (51 centimeters) in shell length and are inhabitants of humid forests and savannas.

The range of the South American yellow-footed tortoise (*Geochelone denticulata*) overlaps some with the range of the red-footed tortoise. However, this species strictly inhabits forest edges and clearings in humid tropical forests. Its range includes southeastern Venezuela through the Caribbean lowlands of Guiana, southward to Brazil, and westward through the Amazon basin to Ecuador, Colombia, northeastern Peru, and northeastern Bolivia. This species also occurs on the island of Trinidad.

Yellow-footed tortoises consume a variety of fruits, leaves, plants, and insects. They have been found in groups consuming fallen fruit beneath wild plum trees.

The manner in which red- and yellow-footed tortoises arrived on the islands they currently inhabit is unclear. Prehistoric dwellers may have brought the tortoises to the islands for food. The tortoises may have arrived naturally, via rafting or other natural phenomenon. Other theories are that early European settlers brought the tortoises or that the wild populations were started by escaped pets.

Like many other chelonians that inhabit the Amazon and Orinoco basins of South America, red- and yellow-footed tortoises are often a source of food. It is common to find these species for sale in marketplaces, either alive or butchered. Many people keep the tortoises in pens and fatten them with ripe plantains until they are deemed suitable for eating. In some areas, indigenous people hunt for the tortoises. The hunters transport as many as a dozen adult tortoises at one time in frame-like backpacks that are constructed from long, wooden poles. Given the weight of adult specimens, this task is not necessarily easy. The load often outweighs the hunter himself.

Lying 250 miles (400 kilometers) off the coast of Mozambique is the island nation of Madagascar. Noted for its wealth of distinctive flora and fauna, Madagascar is the location of four species of endemic tortoises.

Two species of *Geochelone* occur on Madagascar. The radiated tortoise (*G. radiata*) inhabits the dry, southern coast. Although this species has been protected by law since 1960, it is susceptible to habitat loss and collection for food. For most Malagasy, the meat of the radiated tortoise is *faday* ("taboo"). However, such cultural restrictions do not exist for many of the Malagasy who share the tortoises' northwestern and southeastern range.

The ploughshare tortoise or angonoka (*G. yniphora*) is one of the world's most endangered tortoises and is found only in specific locations near Baly Bay in northwestern Madagascar. Captive breeding programs for this species are underway as well as assessments of the remaining amount of suitable habitat for the tortoises.

The common spider tortoise (*Pyxis arachnoides*) is a small tortoise that reaches a maximum length of 6 inches (15 centimeters). It is the only species of tortoise with an anterior hinge on its plastron. Spider tortoises reside in forested areas of southern Madagascar. The flat-shelled spider tortoise (*Pyxis planicauda*) has a somewhat flattened carapace that can reach up to 5 inches (12 centimeters) in length. It occurs in southwestern Madagascar, in a habitat similar to that of the common spider tortoise.

Family Trionychidae
Soft-Shelled Turtles

With fifteen genera and thirty species, the family Trionychidae occurs throughout most of the world. These distinctive turtles have a range that includes North America, Africa, southern and eastern Asia, and the East Indies to New Guinea. Fossil records from the late Jurassic period provide evidence that this family's distribution once included Europe and South America.

The family Trionychidae includes the largest freshwater turtle in the world. The soft-shelled turtles range in size from the petite 12-inch (30-centimeter) Indian flapshell turtle (*Lissemys punctata*) to the gigantic 6.5-foot (2-meter) Shanghai soft-shelled turtle (*Rafetus swinhoei*).

Soft-shelled turtles are flattened and disk-like in their overall appearance. As their common name suggests, they possess a carapace that is covered with a layer of leathery flesh, rather than the more common horny scutes. The number of bones in the carapace is greatly reduced, and the carapace has a flexible posterior edge. Some species demonstrate such a significant reduction of bones that the carapace bulges when the head is in a retracted position.

Within their aquatic realm, soft-shelled turtles are masters. The low-profile shell reduces resistance underwater. Powerful legs and fully webbed feet propel the aerodynamic body, which gives the turtle the ability to swim fast while maneuvering with graceful agility. The long neck has extensive vascularized tissue that allows the soft-shelled turtle to absorb oxygen directly from the water. This characteristic, combined with the snorkel-like nose, lets the turtle remain submerged for considerable amounts of time. While submerged, this turtle waits patiently for prey

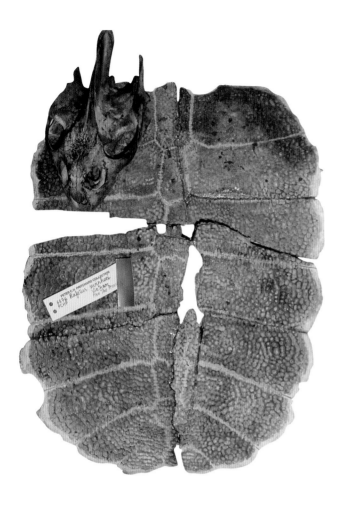

These are the skeletal remains of the rare Shanghai soft-shelled turtle (Rafetus swinhoei). *This species is so rare that only a handful of specimens are available for scientists to examine.*

to venture within reach. Its keen sense of vision and a well-developed sense of smell helps the soft-shell survey its territory for food, danger, and mates.

When they are not basking or actively patrolling the waterways, soft-shelled turtles can be found lying on the bottom of a body of water. Typically, the turtle settles on the bottom and covers itself with sand, fine gravel, or other substrate material until its body is completely concealed. Often, the concealment is so effective that only two eyes betray the buried reptile. When it's completely camouflaged, the turtle waits for an unsuspecting meal to come within striking distance of its cusped jaws. The beaks of soft-shelled turtles are equipped with a sharp-edged cusp that is designed to grasp slippery prey items and cut food into small pieces before swallowing.

Some species of soft-shelled turtles include vegetative matter in their diets. However, this is likely the

result of ingesting vegetative matter while feeding on other prey items. For example, the stomach contents of one soft-shelled turtle I examined revealed that snails were attached to the sides of the plants and suggested that the plants were ingested secondarily. Soft-shelled turtles primarily hunt live prey or opportunistically scavenge dead and decaying animals for food.

Subfamily Cyclanorbinae

The family Trionychidae splits into two subfamilies: Cyclanorbinae and Trionychinae. Members of the subfamily Cyclanorbinae are often referred to as flapshell turtles. This name stems from the presence of femoral flaps that are located on the plastron. When the hind legs are withdrawn, these flaps of skin cover the retracted limbs. It is unclear what protection the flaps offer against predators. Flapshell turtles reach a maximum length of 24 inches (60 centimeters) and have a distribution that includes Africa, India, and southern Asia.

Flapshell turtles are represented by three genera and six species. Four species are endemic to Africa, while the other two occur in India and southern Asia.

Two genera and four species of flapshell turtles are found in a portion of northeastern central Africa and sub-Saharan Africa. The Nubian flapshell turtle (*Cyclanorbis elegans*) has a geographic distribution that includes Sudan westward to Togo. It is known to reach up to 2 feet (60 centimeters) in carapace length. The Senegal flapshell turtle (*Cyclanorbis senegalensis*) has a larger distribution that ranges from Sudan westward through Cameroon to Gabon, Senegal, and Ghana. This species can attain a carapace length of 14 inches (35 centimeters). Both species inhabit marshes, lakes, streams, and slow-moving rivers.

The second genus of flapshell turtles in Africa is *Cycloderma*. Aubry's flapshell turtle (*C. aubryi*) and the Zambezi flapshell (*C. frenatum*) both grow to the size of 22 inches (56 centimeters) in carapace length. Aubrey's flapshell turtle inhabits rivers, ponds, and lakes, while the Zambezi flapshell prefers bodies of water within rainforests.

The Indian flapshell turtle (*Lissemys punctata*) occurs in the Indus and Ganges river drainages of Pakistan, India, Nepal, Bangladesh, as well as Sri Lanka and Nepal. This modestly sized flapshell attains a carapace length of 10 inches (25 centimeters) and

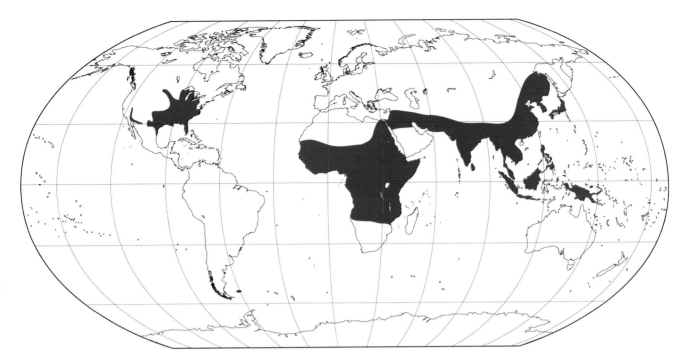

inhabits shallow, quiet water bodies such as canals, rivers, ponds, lakes, and marshes.

The Burmese flapshell turtle (*Lissemys scutata*) occurs in the Irrawaddy and Salween river drainages of Myanmar. Unfortunately, this species has experienced a serious decline in the wild due to pressures from the Asian turtle trade. It is included on the IUCN's red list of endangered species. *L. punctata* aestivate during dry, hot periods and prefers a water body that has a sandy bottom where it can easily burrow during dry conditions.

Subfamily Trionychinae

The second major group of soft-shelled turtles is the subfamily Trionychinae. Unlike the flapshells, these soft-shelled turtles lack the femoral coverings. Trionychinae occur in eastern North America, southern and eastern Asia, the Philippines, Sumatra, and New Guinea. Not only does this subfamily have a larger geographic distribution than Cyclanorbinae, but they attain larger sizes as well.

It is highly probable that the largest freshwater turtle alive today is a soft-shelled turtle. The Shanghai soft-shelled turtle (*Rafetus swinhoei*) has become the focus of many turtle experts. The particular specimen, which many people have become familiar with, resides in Hoan Kiem Lake, Hanoi, Vietnam. Based on estimates, this individual measures 6.6 feet (2 meters) in length and weighs as much as 400 pounds (181 kilograms)! Hopefully, scientists can unravel some of the mysteries surrounding this enigmatic creature before it is too late. Unfortunately, the chances of this turtle finding a mate appear uncertain because there are no known specimens of its kind from this location.

Soft-shelled turtles are one of the most commonly sought species of turtle for human consumption. Although they lack a hardened carapace, these turtles are by no means helpless. When a potentially dangerous situation arises, soft-shelled turtles can make a hasty retreat in the water. If escape is not an option, these turtles can kick and scrape with their clawed feet. They can also extend their long necks with lightning-quick strikes in an attempt to bite their handler. The cusped jaws of soft-shelled turtles can inflict serious injuries to anyone handling one of these turtles without caution. While not as noticeably pungent as many other aquatic turtles, frightened soft-shelled turtles sometimes emit an unpleasant scent when molested.

Many of the details pertaining to the reproductive biology of soft-shelled turtles are still unknown. Observations of smooth soft-shelled turtles (*Apalone mutica*) revealed that following hibernation, males begin to search for females. A male searching for a female investigates the sex by placing his nostrils

*The spiny soft-shelled turtle (*Apalone spinifera*) earned its common name from a row of tubercles at the front of the carapace.*

beneath the carapace of other turtles until a female is located. Mating occurs underwater and at depths that are sufficient for swimming. Females do not always remain motionless while mating; during these occasions, the male will swim alongside the female to continue mating.

When it is time to deposit her eggs, the female soft-shelled turtle selects a suitable location and excavates a flask-shaped nest. Sandy locations are a popular choice. Females deposit as many as 12 to 187 eggs, depending upon the size and species.

Only one species of soft-shelled turtle belonging to the subfamily Trionichynae is found in Africa. The Nile soft-shelled turtle (*Trionyx triunguis*) occurs in rivers, lakes, and ponds throughout most of continental Africa, except for the extreme north and south. These turtles also demonstrate a tolerance for salt water. In fact, thriving populations have been found living off the coast of Turkey. Nile soft-shelled turtles can reach 37 inches (95 centimeters) in length and weigh up to 88 pounds (40 kilograms). This large turtle consumes a wide range of food items. Researchers investigating the diet of Nile soft-

shelled turtles in Nigeria revealed that 22 percent of the general dietary composition was plant matter. The majority of the plant matter was composed of seeds and fruits.

One genus and four species comprise the soft-shelled turtle diversity in North America. In general, North American soft-shelled turtles are moderately sized. The Florida soft-shelled turtle (*Apalone ferox*) attains the largest size at 25 inches (63 centimeters). This species has a distribution that includes southern South Carolina, central Georgia, eastern Alabama, and Florida.

The smooth soft-shelled turtle (*Apalone mutica*) is one of two species inhabiting the central United States and reaches 14 inches (35 centimeters) in carapace length. Unlike its cogener, the spiny soft-shelled turtle (*A. spinifera*), this species lacks tubercles on the anterior portion of its carapace.

The spiny soft-shelled turtle has the widest range of all the North American soft-shelled turtles. This species has a geographic distribution that includes southern Ontario and Quebec, Canada, to northern Florida westward to Montana and southeastern California. It also occurs south of the Rio Grande in Juarez, Coahuila, Nuevo Leon, and Tamaulipas, Mexico.

The population of black spiny soft-shelled turtles (*Apalone spinifera ater*) in Coahuila, Mexico at Cuatro Cienegas has been isolated from any other species of soft-shelled turtle for thousands of years.

Eleven genera and fourteen species of soft-shelled turtles occur in Asia. This region contains the highest amount of soft-shelled turtle diversity. Unfortunately, the many species of Asian soft-shelled turtles are hurdling toward extinction due to the more than 1.3 billion people inhabiting the region.

Like other chelonians, Asian soft-shelled turtles are exploited at a tremendous rate. These turtles are utilized for food, traditional medicine, and pets. In fact, the demand in Asia is so high that many Asian turtle dealers are looking to the United States to fill the insatiable appetite demonstrated for these turtles.

Due to the extirpation of some wild populations, captive breeding efforts are underway to capitalize on the market for these turtles. In some instances, Florida soft-shelled turtles (*Apalone ferox*) have been utilized.

The Asiatic soft-shelled turtle (*Amyda cartilaginea*) lives in muddy streams, rivers, ponds, swamps, and oxbow lakes throughout Vietnam, Sumatra, Myanmar, Laos, Malaysia, and Borneo. The olive gray to brownish green carapace can reach up to 28 inches (70 centimeters) in length. A series of yellow spots bordered by black adorn the carapace of juveniles. The spots fade at the onset of maturity, and adults often display a base coloration of olive.

Large females can lay as many as thirty eggs per breeding cycle that are produced in clutches consisting of four to eight eggs each. The eggs require up to 140 days to hatch. When handled, *A. cartilaginea* is aggressive and does not hesitate to bite. This carnivorous species consumes various aquatic invertebrates, fishes, and amphibians.

The striped narrow-headed soft-shelled turtle (*Chitra chitra*) is the largest of three species representing the genus *Chitra*. This species can grow to an enormous size; adult specimens attain a carapace length of up to 48 inches (122 centimeters). These turtles not only reach a spectacular size, but they possess an incredible amount of strength. Turtle expert Peter C. H. Pritchard and Indonesian herpetologist Frank Yuwono witnessed a vivid demonstration of this turtle's strength. Four professional turtle hunters set out searching for a striped giant soft-shell by probing with sharpened bamboo poles beneath overhanging riverbanks. To avoid the viscous bites these turtles can deliver, the hunters pinned the specimen down and then secured the turtle for capture. However, in this instance, the pinned turtle swam away with all four hunters in tow for some 330 feet (100 meters). Later, the turtle broke or removed all of the spears and swam away.

C. chitra has a geographic distribution that includes the Mae Klong River system of western Thailand. This species is endangered due to habitat loss from the construction of dams, mining of sand, pollution, and human consumption for food, medicine, and pets.

The Malayan soft-shelled turtle (*Dogania subplana*) is a monotypic species with a range that includes southern Myanmar, Malaysia, and Indonesia. Reaching a carapace length of 14 inches (35 centimeters), this species occurs in fast-flowing clear streams that have rocky bottoms. When frightened, *Dogania* takes advantage of its flat, flexible shell to hide beneath submerged rocks. Of all the turtles in the world, the Malayan soft-shell possesses the most flexible carapace. The sutures of its carapace are not joined, providing an incredible amount of pliability.

Dogania is a curious-looking species of soft-shell. The edges of the carapace are straight, the head is large, and the nose is long.

The wattle-necked soft-shelled turtle (*Palea steindachneri*) is a medium-sized species measuring up to 17 inches (43 centimeters) in carapace length. Wattle-necks have a geographic distribution that includes southeastern China and Vietnam.

The Chinese soft-shelled turtle (*Pelodiscus sinensis*) has been found almost everywhere in Southeast Asia. Specimens can reach a carapace length of 10 inches (25 centimeters). The natural range of this species includes central and southern China, Hainan Island, Vietnam, Taiwan, Japan, and Timor. Chinese and Japanese immigrants introduced this species, as well as *P. steindachneri*, to the Hawaiian Islands of Kauai and Oahu during the mid to late 1800s.

The Burmese peacock soft-shelled turtle (*Nilssonia formosa*) is a monotypic species that measures up to 16 inches (40 centimeters) in carapace length. This species has a restricted range within the Irrawaddy-Salween River basin of Myanmar.

While the Shanghai soft-shelled turtle (*Rafetus swinhoei*) has earned the distinction of the largest

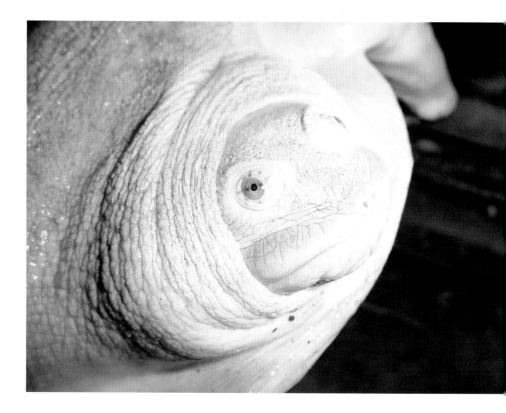

species of freshwater turtle in the world, Cantor's giant soft-shelled turtle (*Pelochelys cantori*) is a close contender. Specimens can grow to 51 inches (129 centimeters) in carapace length. Cantor's giant soft-shell has a range that includes India to southern China, the Malaysian Peninsula, and southern New Guinea. Throughout its range, *P. cantori* occupies rivers as well as the brackish waters of coastal estuaries. There have even been reports of specimens captured at sea. This species is endangered due to consumption for food and habitat loss.

Two species of giant soft-shelled turtles occur in New Guinea. The northern New Guinea giant soft-shelled turtle (*Pelochelys signifera*) is found in the lowlands of northern New Guinea. The lowlands of southern New Guinea provide habitat for the Asian giant soft-shelled turtle (*Pelochelys bibroni*).

Cradled between China, Nepal, and Pakistan is the subcontinent of India; west of India is Pakistan and the Middle East. This region is home to four genera and seven species of soft-shelled turtles.

Soft-shelled turtles around the world are often eaten by people. However, at least one turtle species from India is known to eat people.

The Indian soft-shelled turtle (*Aspideretes gangeticus*) has gained a modest amount of notoriety for some of its scavenging habits. For many Hindis, the Ganges River is not only a natural watercourse but also a sacred location. The Ganges is where many Hindis cremate their dead. Some of the bodies are burned on the banks, while others are sent adrift on floating pyres.

It is interesting to consider the intuitive nature of a creature such as the Indian soft-shelled turtle. There have been published accounts of these turtles consuming the unburned portions of corpses from floating pyres. However, these turtles do not restrict their culinary pursuits to floating morsels in the river. One specimen was observed on land tearing flesh off a corpse while it was still burning. The flames even licked and scorched the carapace of the turtle. Undeterred by the conditions surrounding its lurid feast, the turtle played his role as part of nature's clean-up crew.

As if corpse scavenging was not enough to earn a less-than-positive reputation, consider the example of a male bather who had his penis bitten off by a passing Indian soft-shelled turtle!

The Indian soft-shelled turtle has a distribution that ranges from Pakistan through southern Nepal and northern India to Bangladesh. Within this range, Indian soft-shelled turtles occur in the drainages of the Ganges, Indus, and Mahanadi rivers. *A. gangeticus* attains a respectable size of 28 inches (70 centimeters) in shell length.

Within the Tigris and Euphrates river basins of southeastern Turkey, northeastern Syria, Iraq, and southwestern Iran, the Euphrates soft-shelled turtle (*Rafetus euphraticus*) holds onto a precarious existence in a rapidly changing environment. Damming projects along the Tigris and Euphrates have rendered much of their range uninhabitable.

The Euphrates soft-shell has a dark olive green carapace and reaches up to 26 inches (68 centimeters) in length. The species is known by a few interesting names. The Kurds refer to this species as "ball sucker," while the Turks use the name "scrotum snatcher." These labels leave little to the imagination as to how the Euphrates soft-shell earned its nicknames.

One of the most widespread soft-shelled turtles in India is the Indian flapshell turtle (*Lissemys punctata*). Reaching 14 inches (35 centimeters) in carapace length, this species adapts to a variety of aquatic habitats and occurs in India, Sri Lanka, western Myanmar, and Bangladesh. Although it is sometimes seen basking amid aquatic vegetation, this species prefers to remain underwater and partially submerged in the mud. From this vantage point, it can strike at passing prey.

Indian flapshell turtles make considerable overland migrations during the rainy season. These migrations may be a reaction to the massive amounts of rainfall in their range, which can make it a challenge for them to locate a suitable nesting location.

L. punctata is an opportunistic feeder that consumes a variety of aquatic invertebrates, as well as fish and amphibians. Aquatic plants make up some of the diet; however, the ingestion of vegetative material may be coincidental with the ingestion of prey. When handled, this species releases a noxious yellowish substance from glands on the side of the body.

Appendix
Taxonomy of Turtles

A general overview of the living turtles of the world, including scientific and common English names

Family Carettochelyidae

Carettochelys insculpta (Fly River turtle or pig-nosed turtle), Ramsay, 1886

Family Chelidae

Acanthochelys macrocephala (Pantanal swamp turtle), Rhodin, Mettermeier, and McMorris, 1984

Acanthochelys pallidipectoris (Chaco side-necked turtle), Freidberg, 1945

Acanthochelys radiolata (Brazilian radiolated swamp turtle), Mikan, 1820

Acanthochelys spixii (spiny-necked turtle), Duméril and Bibron, 1835

Batrachemys dahli (Dahl's toad-headed turtle), Zangerl and Medem, 1958

*Common snake-necked turtle (*Chelodina longicollis*)*

Batrachemys heliostemma (Amazon toad-headed turtle), McCord, Joseph-Ouni, and Lamar, 2001

Batrachemys nasuta (common toad-headed turtle), Schweigger, 1812

Batrachemys raniceps (black-lined toad-headed turtle), Gray, 1855

Batrachemys tuberculata (tuberculate toad-headed turtle), Luederwaldt, 1926

Batrachemys zuliae (Zulia toad-headed turtle), Pritchard and Trebbau, 1984

Bufocephala vanderhaegei (Vanderhaege's toad-headed turtle), Bour, 1973

Chelodina canni (Cann's snake-necked turtle), McCord and Thompson, 2002

Chelodina kuchlingi (Kuchling's snake-necked turtle), Cann, 1997

Chelodina longicollis (common snake-necked turtle), Shaw, 1794

Chelodina mccordi (McCord's snake-necked turtle), Rhodin, 1994

Chelodina novaeguineae (New Guinea snake-necked turtle), Boulenger, 1888

Chelodina oblonga (narrow-breasted snake-necked turtle), Gray, 1841

Chelodina pritchardi (Pritchard's snake-necked turtle), Rhodin, 1994

Chelodina reimanni (Reimann's snake-necked turtle), Philippen and Grossmann, 1990

Chelodina siebenrocki (Siebenrock's snake-necked turtle), Werner, 1901

Chelodina steindachneri (Steindachner's snake-necked turtle), Siebenrock, 1914

Chelus fimbriatus (matamata), Schneider, 1783

Elseya dentata (Victoria River snapping turtle), Gray, 1863

Elseya georgesi (George's snapping turtle), Cann, 1997

Elseya irwini (Irwin's snapping turtle), Cann, 1997

Elseya latisternum (Serrated snapping turtle), Gray, 1867

Elseya lavarackorum (gulf snapping turtle), White and Archer, 1994

Elseya novaeguineae (New Guinea snapping turtle), Meyer, 1874

Elseya purvisi (Purvis' snapping turtle), Wells and Wellington, 1985

Elseya schultzei (northern New Guinea snapping turtle), Vogt, 1911

Elusor macrurus (Mary River turtle), Cann and Legler, 1994

Emydura australis (Australian big-headed turtle), Gray, 1841

Emydura krefftii (Krefft's River turtle), Gray, 1871

Emydura macquarii (Murray River turtle), Gray, 1831

Emydura signata (Brisbane short-necked turtle), Ahl, 1932

Emydura subglobosa (red-bellied short-necked turtle), Hrefft, 1876

Emydura tanybaraga (northern yellow-faced turtle), Cann, 1997

Emydura victoriae (Victoria short-necked turtle), Gray, 1842

Hydromedusa maximiliani (Brazilian snake-necked turtle), Mikan, 1820

Hydromedusa tectifera (South American snake-necked turtle), Cope, 1869

Macrochelodina burrungandjii (Arnhem snake-necked turtle), Thomson, Kennett, and Georges, 2000

Macrochelodina expansa (giant snake-necked turtle), Gray, 1857

Macrochelodina parkeri (Parker's snake-necked turtle), Rhodin and Mittermeier, 1976

Macrochelodina rugosa (northern Australian snake-necked turtle), Ogilby, 1890

Mesoclemmys gibba (Gibba turtle), Schweigger, 1812

Phrynops geoffroanus (Geoffroy's side-necked turtle), Schweigger, 1812

Phrynops hilarii (Hilaire's side-necked turtle), Duméril and Bibron, 1835

Phrynops tuberosus (Cotinga River toad-headed turtle), Peters, 1870

Phrynops williamsi (William's side-necked turtle), Rhodin and Mittermeier, 1983

Platemys platycephala (twist-necked turtle), Schneider, 1792

Pseudemydura umbrina (western swamp turtle), Siebenrock, 1901

Ranacephala hogei (Hoge's side-necked turtle), Mertens, 1967

Rheodytes leukops (Fitzroy River turtle), Legler and Cann, 1980

Rhinemys rufipes (red side-necked turtle), Spix, 1824

*Alligator snapping turtle (*Macrochelys temminckii*)*

Family Cheloniidae

Caretta caretta (loggerhead sea turtle), Linnaeus, 1758

Chelonia mydas agassizi (black sea turtle), Linnaeus, 1758

Chelonia mydas mydas (green sea turtle), Linnaeus, 1758

Eretmochelys imbricata (hawksbill sea turtle), Linnaeus, 1766

Lepidochelys kempii (Kemp's ridley sea turtle), Garman, 1880

Lepidochelys olivacea (olive ridley sea turtle), Escholtz, 1829

Natator depressus (flatback sea turtle), Garman, 1880

Family Chelydridae

Chelydra serpentina (common snapping turtle), Linnaeus, 1758

Macrochelys temminckii (alligator snapping turtle), Harlan, 1835

Family Dermatemyidae

Dermatemys mawii (Central American river turtle), Gray, 1847

Family Dermochelyidae

Dermochelys coriacea (leatherback sea turtle), Vandelli, 1761

Family Emydidae

Actinemys marmorata (Pacific pond turtle), Baird and Girard, 1852

Chrysemys picta (painted turtle), Schneider, 1783

Clemmys guttata (spotted turtle), Schneider, 1792

Clemmys muhlenbergii (bog turtle), Schoepff, 1801

Deirochelys reticularia (chicken turtle), Latrielle, 1801

Emydoidea blandingii (Blanding's turtle), Holbrook, 1838

Emys orbicularis (European pond turtle), Linnaeus, 1758

Glyptemys insculpta (North American wood turtle), LeConte, 1829

Graptemys barbouri (Barbour's map turtle), Carr and Marchand, 1942

Graptemys caglei (Cagle's map turtle), Haynes and McKown, 1974

Graptemys ernsti (Escambia map turtle), Lovich and McCoy, 1992

Graptemys flavimaculata (yellow-blotched map turtle), Cagle, 1954

Graptemys geographica (common map turtle), LeSuer, 1817

Graptemys gibbonsi (Gibbon's map turtle), Lovich and McCoy, 1992

Graptemys nigrinoda (black-knobbed map turtle), Cagle, 1954

Graptemys oculifera (ringed map turtle), Baur, 1890

Graptemys ouachitensis (Ouachita map turtle), Cagle, 1953

Graptemys pseudogeographica (false map turtle), Gray, 1831

Graptemys pulchra (Alabama map turtle), Baur, 1893

Graptemys versa (Texas map turtle), Stejneger, 1925

Malaclemys terrapin (diamondback terrapin), Schoepff, 1793

Pseudemys alabamensis (Alabama red-bellied turtle), Baur, 1893

Pseudemys concinna (river cooter), LeConte, 1829

Pseudemys gorzugi (Rio Grande cooter), Ward, 1984

Pseudemys nelsoni (Florida red-bellied cooter), Carr, 1938

Pseudemys peninsularis (peninsula cooter), Carr, 1938

Pseudemys rubriventris (American red-bellied turtle), LeConte, 1829

Pseudemys suwanniensis (Suwannee River cooter), Carr, 1937

Pseudemys texana (Texas cooter), Baur, 1893

Terrapene carolina (common box turtle), Linnaeus, 1758

Terrapene coahuila (Coahuilan box turtle), Schmidt and Owens, 1944

Terrapene nelsoni (spotted box turtle), Stejneger, 1925

Terrapene ornata (ornate box turtle), Agassiz, 1857

Trachemys adiutrix (Brazilian slider), Vonzolini, 1995

Trachemys decorata (Hispaniolan slider), Barbour and Carr, 1940

Trachemys decussata (North Antillean slider), Gray, 1831

Indochinese box turtle (Cuora galbinifrons)

Trachemys dorbigni (Orbigny's slider), Duméril and Bibron, 1835

Trachemys gaigeae (Big Bend slider), Hartweg, 1939

Trachemys scripta (common slider), Schoepff, 1792

Trachemys stejnegeri (Central Antillean slider), Schmidt, 1928

Trachemys terrapen (Jamaican slider), Bonnaterre, 1789

Family Geoemydidae

Batagur baska (river terrapin), Gray, 1855

Callagur borneoensis (painted terrapin), Schlegel and Müller, 1844

Chinemys megalocephala (Chinese broad-headed pond turtle), Fang, 1934

Chinemys nigricans (red-necked pond turtle), Gray, 1834

Chinemys reevesii (Reeves' turtle), Gray, 1831

Cuora amboinensis (Southeast Asian box turtle), Daudin, 1802

Cuora aurocapitata (yellow-headed box turtle), Luo and Zong, 1988

Cuora flavomarginata (yellow-margined box turtle), Gray, 1863

Cuora galbinifrons (Indochinese box turtle), Bourret, 1939

Cuora mccordi (McCord's box turtle), Ernst, 1988

Cuora pani (Pan's box turtle), Song, 1984

Cuora trifasciata (Chinese three-striped box turtle), Bell, 1825

Cuora yunnanensis (Yunnan box turtle), Boulenger, 1906

Cuora zhoui (Zhou's box turtle), Zhao, 1990

Cyclemys atripons (striped leaf turtle), Iverson and McCord, 1997

Cyclemys dentata (Asian leaf turtle), Gray, 1831

Cyclemys oldhami (Oldham's leaf turtle), Gray, 1863

Cyclemys tcheponensis (stripe-necked leaf turtle), Bourret, 1939

Geoclemys hamiltonii (spotted pond turtle), Gray, 1831

Geoemyda japonica (Japanese leaf turtle), Fan, 1931

Geoemyda silvatica (Cochin forest cane turtle), Henderson, 1912

Geoemyda spengleri (black-breasted leaf turtle), Gmelin, 1789

Hardella thurjii (crowned river turtle), Gray, 1831

Heosemys depressa (Arakan forest turtle), Anderson, 1875

Heosemys grandis (giant Asian pond turtle), Gray, 1860

Heosemys leytensis (Philippine pond turtle), Taylor, 1920

Heosemys spinosa (spiny turtle), Gray, 1831

Hieremys annandalii (yellow-headed temple turtle), Boulenger, 1903

Kachuga dhongoka (three-striped roofed turtle), Gray, 1835

Kachuga kachuga (red-crowned roofed turtle), Gray, 1831

Kachuga smithii (brown roofed turtle), Gray, 1863

Kachuga sylhetensis (Assam roofed turtle), Jerdon, 1870

Kachuga tecta (Indian roofed turtle), Gray, 1831

Kachuga tentoria (Indian tent turtle), Gray, 1834

Kachuga trivittata (Burmese roofed turtle), Duméril and Bibron, 1835

Leucocephalon yuwonoi (Sulawesi forest turtle), McCord, Iverson, and Boedai, 1995

Malayemys subtrijuga (Malayan snail-eating turtle), Lindholm, 1931

Mauremys annamensis (Annam leaf turtle), Siebenrock, 1903

Mauremys caspica (Caspian turtle), Gmelin, 1774

Mauremys iversoni (Fujian pond turtle), Pritchard and McCord, 1991

Mauremys japonica (Japanese pond turtle), Temminck and Schlegel, 1835

Mauremys leprosa (Mediterranean turtle), Schweigger, 1812

Mauremys mutica (yellow pond turtle), Cantor, 1842

Melanochelys tricarinata (tricarinate hill turtle), Blyth, 1856

Melanochelys trijuga (Indian black turtle), Schweigger, 1812

Morenia ocellata (Burmese eyed turtle), Duméril and Bibron, 1835

Morenia petersi (Indian eyed turtle), Anderson, 1879

Notochelys platynota (Malayan flat-shelled turtle), Gray, 1834

Ocadia philippeni (Philippen's stripe-necked turtle), McCord and Iverson, 1992

Ocadia sinensis (Chinese stripe-necked turtle), Gray, 1834

Orlitia borneensis (Malaysian giant turtle), Gray, 1873

Pyxidea mouhotii (keeled box turtle), Gray, 1862

Rhinoclemmys annulata (brown wood turtle), Gray, 1860

Rhinoclemmys areolata (furrowed wood turtle), Duméril and Duméril, 1851

Rhinoclemmys diademata (Maracaibo wood turtle), Mertens, 1954

Rhinoclemmys funerea (black wood turtle), Cope, 1875

Rhinoclemmys melanosterna (Colombian wood turtle), Gray, 1861

Rhinoclemmys nasuta (large-nosed wood turtle), Boulenger, 1902

Rhinoclemmys pulcherrima (painted wood turtle), Gray, 1855

Rhinoclemmys punctularia (spot-legged turtle), Daudin, 1802

Rhinoclemmys rubida (Mexican spotted wood turtle), Cope, 1869

Sacalia bealei (Beal's eyed turtle), Gray, 1831

Sacalia pseudocellata (false-eyed turtle), Iverson and McCord, 1992

Sacalia quadriocellata (four-eyed turtle), Siebenrock, 1903

Siebenrockiella crassicollis (black marsh turtle), Gray, 1831

Family Kinosternidae

Kinosternon abaxillare (Central Chiapas mud turtle), Baur, 1925

Kinosternon acutum (Tabasco mud turtle), Gray, 1831

Kinosternon alamosae (Alamos mud turtle), Berry and Legler, 1980

Kinosternon angustipons (narrow-bridged mud turtle), Legler, 1965

Kinosternon baurii (striped mud turtle), Garman, 1891

Kinosternon chimalhuaca (Jalisco mud turtle), Berry, Seidel, and Iverson, 1997

Kinosternon creaseri (Creaser's mud turtle), Hartweg, 1934

Kinosternon cruentatum (red-cheeked mud turtle), Baur, 1925

Kinosternon dunni (Dunn's mud turtle), Schmidt, 1947

Kinosternon flavescens (yellow mud turtle), Agassiz, 1857

Kinosternon herrerai (Herrera's mud turtle), Stejneger, 1925

Kinosternon hirtipes (Mexican rough-footed mud turtle), Wagler, 1830

Kinosternon integrum (Mexican mud turtle), LeConte, 1854

Kinosternon leucostomum (white-lipped mud turtle), Duméril and Bibron, 1851

Kinosternon oaxacae (Oaxaca mud turtle), Berry and Iverson, 1980

Kinosternon scorpioides (scorpion mud turtle), Linnaeus, 1766

Kinosternon sonoriense (Sonora mud turtle), LeConte, 1854

Kinosternon spurrelli (western Colombian mud turtle), Boulenger 1913

Kinosternon subrubrum (common mud turtle), Bonnaterre, 1789

Sternotherus carinatus (razor-backed musk turtle), Gray, 1855

Sternotherus depressus (flattened musk turtle), Tinkle and Webb, 1955

Sternotherus minor (loggerhead musk turtle), Agassiz, 1857

Sternotherus odoratus (common musk turtle), Latrielle, 1801

Family Pelomedusidae

Pelomedusa subrufa (helmeted turtle), Bonnaterre, 1789

Pelusios adansonii (Adanson's mud turtle), Schweigger, 1812

Pelusios bechuanicus (Okavango mud turtle), FitzSimmons, 1932

Pelusios broadleyi (Turkana mud turtle), Bour, 1986

Pelusios carinatus (African keeled mud turtle), Laurent, 1956

Pelusios castaneus (West African mud turtle), Schweigger, 1812

Pelusios castanoides (yellow-bellied mud turtle), Hewitt, 1931

Pelusios chapini (Central African mud turtle), Laurent, 1965

Pelusios cupulatta (Ivory Coast mud turtle), Bour and Maran, 2003

Pelusios gabonensis (African forest turtle), Duméril, 1856

Pelusios marani (Maran's mud turtle), Bour, 2000

Pelusios nanus (African dwarf mud turtle), Laurent, 1956

Pelusios niger (West African black mud turtle), Duméril and Bibron, 1835

Pelusios rhodesianus (variable mud turtle), Hewitt, 1927

Pelusios seychellensis (Seychelles mud turtle), Siebenrock, 1906

Pelusios sinuatus (East African serrated mud turtle), Smith, 1838

Pelusios subniger (East African black mud turtle), Bonnaterre, 1789

Pelusios upembae (Upemba mud turtle), Broadley, 1981

Pelusios williamsi (William's mud turtle), Laurent, 1965

Family Platysternidae

Platysternon megacephalum (big-headed turtle), Gray, 1831

Family Podocnemidae

Erymnochelys madagascariensis (Madagascan big-headed turtle), Grandidier, 1867

Peltocephalus dumerilianus (big-headed Amazon River turtle), Schweigger, 1812

Podocnemis erythrocephala (red-headed river turtle), Spix, 1824

Podocnemis expansa (South American river turtle), Schweigger, 1812

Podocnemis lewyana (Magdalena River turtle), Duméril, 1852

Podocnemis sextuberculata (six-tubercled Amazon River turtle), Cornalia, 1849

Podocnemis unifilis (yellow-spotted river turtle), Troschel, 1848

Podocnemis vogli (savanna side-necked turtle), Müller, 1935

Family Staurotypidae

Claudius angustatus (narrow-bridged musk turtle), Cope, 1865

Staurotypus salvinii (Pacific Coast giant musk turtle), Gray, 1864

Staurotypus triporcatus (Mexican giant musk turtle), Wiegmann, 1828

Family Testudinidae

Chersina angulata (South African bowsprit tortoise), Schweigger, 1812

Dipsochelys arnoldi (Arnold's or Seychelles saddle-backed tortoise), Bour, 1982

Dipsochelys dussumieri (Aldabra giant tortoise), Gray, 1831

Dipsochelys hololissa (Seychelles giant tortoise), Günther, 1877

Geochelone carbonaria (red-footed tortoise), Spix, 1824

Geochelone chilensis (Chaco tortoise), Gray, 1870

Geochelone denticulata (South American yellow-footed tortoise), Linnaeus, 1766

Geochelone elegans (Indian star tortoise), Schoepff, 1794

Geochelone nigra (Galápagos tortoise), Quoy and Gaimard, 1824

Geochelone pardalis (leopard tortoise), Bell, 1828

Geochelone platynota (Burmese star tortoise), Blyth, 1863

Geochelone radiata (radiated tortoise), Shaw, 1802

Geochelone sulcata (African spurred tortoise), Miller, 1779

Geochelone yniphora (ploughshare tortoise or angonoka), Vaillant, 1885

Gopherus agassizii (desert tortoise), Cooper, 1863

Gopherus berlandieri (Berlandier's tortoise), Agassiz, 1857

Gopherus flavomarginatus (bolson tortoise), Legler, 1959

Gopherus polyphemus (gopher tortoise), Daudin, 1802

Homopus areolatus (beaked cape tortoise), Thunberg, 1787

Homopus boulengeri (Boulenger's cape tortoise), Duerden, 1906

Homopus femoralis (Karoo cape tortoise), Boulenger, 1888

Homopus signatus (speckled padloper), Gmelin, 1789

Indotestudo elongata (elongated tortoise), Blyth, 1853

Indotestudo forstenii (Travancore tortoise), Schlegel and Müller, 1844

Kinixys belliana (Bell's hinge-back tortoise), Gray, 1831

Kinixys erosa (serrated hinge-back tortoise), Schweigger, 1812

Kinixys homeana (Home's hinge-back tortoise), Bell, 1827

Kinixys lobatsiana (Lobatse hinge-back tortoise), Power, 1927

Kinixys natalensis (Natal hinge-back tortoise), Hewitt, 1935

Kinixys spekii (Speke's hinge-back tortoise), Hailey and Loveridge, 1997

Malacochersus tornieri (African pancake tortoise), Siebenrock, 1903

Manouria emys (Asian brown tortoise), Schlegel and Müller, 1844

Manouria impressa (impressed tortoise), Günther, 1882

Psammobates geometricus (geometric tortoise), Linnaeus, 1758

Psammobates oculifer (serrated tortoise), Kuhl, 1820

Psammobates tentorius (tent tortoise), Bell, 1828

Pyxis arachnoides (common spider tortoise), Bell, 1827

Pyxis planicauda (flat-shelled spider tortoise), Grandidier, 1867

Testudo antakyensis (Antakyan tortoise), Perälä, 1996

Testudo flavominimaralis (yellow miniature tortoise), Highfield and Martin, 1990

Testudo graeca (spur-thighed tortoise), Linnaeus, 1758

Testudo hermanni (Herman's tortoise), Gmelin, 1789

Testudo horsfieldii (Central Asian tortoise), Gray, 1844

Testudo kleinmanni (Egyptian tortoise), Lortet, 1883

Testudo marginata (marginated tortoise), Schoepff, 1792

Testudo werneri (Mediterranean tortoise), Perälä, 2001

Family Trionychidae

Amyda cartilaginea (Asiatic soft-shelled turtle), Boddaert, 1770

Apalone ferox (Florida soft-shelled turtle), Schneider, 1783

Apalone mutica (smooth soft-shelled turtle), LeSuer, 1827

Apalone spinifera (spiny soft-shelled turtle), LeSuer, 1827

Aspideretes gangeticus (Indian soft-shelled turtle), Cuvier, 1825

Aspideretes hurum (Indian peacock soft-shelled turtle), Gray, 1831

Aspideretes leithii (Leith's soft-shelled turtle), Gray, 1872

Aspideretes nigricans (black soft-shelled turtle), Anderson, 1875

Chitra chitra (striped narrow-headed soft-shelled turtle), Hamilton, 1831

Chitra indica (narrow-headed soft-shelled turtle), Gray, 1831

Chitra vandijki (Myanmar narrow-headed soft-shelled turtle), McCord and Pritchard, 2003

Cyclanorbis elegans (Nubian flapshell turtle), Gray, 1869

Cyclanorbis senegalensis (Senegal flapshell turtle), Duméril and Bibron, 1835

Cycloderma aubryi (Aubry's flapshell turtle), Duméril, 1856

Cycloderma frenatum (Zambezi flapshell turtle), Peters, 1854

Dogania subplana (Malayan soft-shelled turtle), Geoffroy Saint Hilaire, 1809

Lissemys punctata (Indian flapshell turtle), Bonnaterre, 1789

Lissemys scutata (Burmese flapshell turtle), Peters, 1868

Nilssonia formosa (Burmese peacock soft-shelled turtle), Gray, 1869

Palea steindachneri (wattle-necked soft-shelled turtle), Siebenrock, 1906

Pelochelys bibroni (Asian giant soft-shelled turtle), Owen, 1853

Pelochelys cantori (Cantor's giant soft-shelled turtle), Gray, 1864

Pelochelys signifera (northern New Guinea giant soft-shelled turtle), Webb, 2002

Pelodiscus sinensis (Chinese soft-shelled turtle), Wiegmann, 1835

Rafetus euphraticus (Euphrates soft-shelled turtle), Daudin, 1802

Rafetus swinhoei (Shanghai soft-shelled turtle), Gray, 1873

Trionyx triunguis (Nile soft-shelled turtle), Forsskål, 1775

Remember to always drive with caution and keep an eye for creatures crossing the road while in turtle country.

Conservation Organizations

Asian Turtle Conservation Network: www.asianturtlenetwork.org

Asian Turtle Consortium: www.asianturtle.org

Box Turtle Partnership of Texas: www.btpt.org

Chelonian Research Foundation: www.chelonian.org

Madras Crocodile Bank Trust: www.madrascrocodilebank.org

Nature Protection Trust of Seychelles: http://members.aol.com/jstgerlach

New York Turtle and Tortoise Society: www.nytts.org

Savannah River Ecology Lab: www.uga.edu/~srel

Seaturtle.org: www.seaturtle.org

Turtle Conservation Fund: www.chelonian.org/tcf

Turtle Survival Alliance: www.turtlesurvival.org

Index

About the Author

Author Carl J. Franklin (right) in the field, turning rocks in search of snakes.

Author Carl J. Franklin is the biological curator and collections manager of the Amphibian and Reptile Diversity Research Center at the University of Texas at Arlington. He has published several articles on herpetoculture and herpetology in popular and technical formats. Carl has suffered a lifelong affliction relating to an insatiable curiosity for amphibians and reptiles. In an attempt to satiate this boundless herpetological enthusiasm, Carl is subjected to inordinate amounts of time in the field collecting specimens from the United States, Mexico, and Central and South America. He currently resides with his wife, son, dogs, and turtles in Grand Prairie, Texas.